P9-DWE-822

Broadcasting Careers

WITHDRAWN

OPPORTUNITIES

in

Broadcasting Careers

REVISED EDITION

ELMO I. ELLIS

VGM Career Books

New York Chicago San Francisco Lisbon London Madrid Mexico City
Milan New Delhi San Juan Seoul Singapore Sydney Toronto

The McGraw·Hill Companies

Library of Congress Cataloging-in-Publication Data

Ellis, Elmo Israel.
    Opportunities in broadcasting careers / by Elmo I. Ellis.— Rev. ed.
        p.   cm. — (VGM opportunities series)
      ISBN 0-07-143722-3
      1. Broadcasting—Vocational guidance.   I. Title.   II. Series.

   HE8689.6.E43   2004
   384.54'023'73—dc22   2004005225

2 3 4 5 6 7 8 9 0   DOC/DOC   0 9 8 7 6 5

ISBN 0-07-143722-3

Interior design by Rattray Design

McGraw-Hill books are available at special quantity discounts to use as premiums and sales promotions, or for use in corporate training programs. For more information, please write to the Director of Special Sales, Professional Publishing, McGraw-Hill, Two Penn Plaza, New York, NY 10121-2298. Or contact your local bookstore.

This book is printed on acid-free paper.

CONTENTS

Foreword

As the multimedia universe continues to evolve, institutions and individuals are challenged to adapt to new methods of interactive communication. Conventional analog radio, TV, and cable have been integrated into new forms of digital broadcasting and narrowcasting. In this age of computerized information systems, new careers in electronic media have emerged.

What a splendid experience it is to explore new broadcast career opportunities with Elmo Ellis, one of the nation's most renowned and respected broadcast professionals. Ellis is a recognized expert on radio and television journalism in the Southeast and an authority on programming and management practices.

If you are considering a career in broadcasting, the tools you will need are found in these pages. What jobs are out there? How much preparation is required? What technical skills are most important? How much money can one expect to make? Ellis draws from his extensive background to answer these and many other questions for those who want to become communicators.

This book will help students in high schools, universities, and community colleges who want to learn about the many job opportunities that electronic media convergence has created, as well as the jobs it has eliminated. It is also an excellent resource for those who are already in the industry and wish to explore new opportunities.

To anyone else who seeks a better understanding of broadcasting and what it has to offer, I say, "Read this book!"

E. Culpepper Clark
Dean
College of Communication and Information Sciences
The University of Alabama

Acknowledgments

I AM INDEBTED to many broadcasters, educators, and electronic media professionals whose generous contributions made this book possible. They include: James W. Wesley Jr., former president, Patterson Broadcasting Corp.; Michael McDougald, president, McDougald Broadcasting; Bill Sanders, president emeritus, and Lanny Finch, president, Georgia Association of Broadcasters; Dr. Loren Ghiglione, dean and professor, Medill School of Journalism; Dr. Linda Matthews, vice provost and director of university libraries, Emory University; John Holliman, former CNN national correspondent; Lynda Stewart, Betsy Stone, and David Scott, Cox Enterprises; Richard Warner, founder and CEO, What's Up Interactive; Bryan Moffett, editorial director, Radio-Television News Directors Association and Foundation; Robert Alter, vice chairman, Cable Television Advertising Bureau; Dr. Barry Sherman, former director, Peabody Awards, University of Georgia; Dr. Culpepper Clark and Dr. Jennings Bryant, College of Communication and Information Sciences, University of Alabama; Pamela S. Beaird, former director of financial aid, Oglethorpe University; Richard Ducey, George Barber, and Michael D. McKinley, National Association of Broadcasters; Mike Mahone, executive vice president, Radio Advertising Bureau; Bill Israel, professor of journalism, University of Massachusetts; and the editors of *Advertising Age* and *Broadcasting and Cable Yearbook*.

Most of all, I owe heartfelt thanks to my beloved wife, Ruth, who gave me unstinting assistance, nourishment, and encouragement during the preparation of this manuscript.

1

THE NEW WORLD OF BROADCASTING

THANKS TO AN avalanche of news and information that flows into homes and offices from a multitude of broadcasting and narrowcasting sources, those with access to digital technology are better equipped than ever before to remain current on activities all over the globe.

During most of the twentieth century, broadcasters in radio, television, and cable transmitted sights and sounds to millions of listeners and viewers. Today, new forms of interactive communications have emerged and grown in popularity across the expanding multimedia universe.

Digital technology, satellites, fiber optics, lasers, and other sophisticated equipment have created so many options for viewing, listening, and personal expression that you may wonder whether conventional radio and television media will continue to exist and serve the public. The answer is yes, but not without heavy investment in digital devices and interactive services.

Fortunately, interactive media growth has created businesses, generated jobs, and sparked creativity. Windows of opportunity have opened for many talented communicators including journalists, graphic artists, digital specialists, and salespeople.

The Communication Challenge

Despite its many benefits, the communication process is complicated and often creates more problems than it solves. Whether broadcasting to an audience of millions or quietly talking with one person, communication requires collaboration to accurately convey meaning. To communicate effectively, you should meet these requirements:

1. Understand the various ways in which people communicate—accurately and inaccurately, rationally and emotionally, purposefully and unknowingly—with words, signs, symbols, sights, sounds, silence, and mannerisms
2. Learn to observe, listen, speak, write, and spell with a high degree of competence, empathy, clarity, and perception
3. Master the tools of personal and mass communications and become adept at using state-of-the-art technology
4. Acquire general and specific knowledge that will enable you to analyze and interpret facts, opinions, and theories
5. Know how and where to obtain information and how to refine it into useful knowledge
6. Initiate and maintain a lifelong learning program for personal and professional development that will enable you to meet the constantly changing demands of a communications career

The Big Picture

There are more than six hundred million working radios in the United States that are found in virtually every home, automobile, and place of business. Some 12,200 AM and FM radio stations are on the air, and the Federal Communications Commission (FCC) continues to issue construction permits for more outlets.

About 1,600 commercial and educational TV stations provide entertainment and information to the nation's households. In addition, two thousand very-high frequency (VHF) and ultra-high frequency (UHF) low-power television stations and some eight thousand FM, VHF, and UHF translators and booster stations exist.

Most broadcasting stations and cable systems in the United States are commercial operations engaged in selling programs and spot announcements to advertisers. Educational and noncommercial facilities, which are usually owned and managed by educational and religious institutions, do not sell advertising time. They are, however, allowed to solicit limited amounts of financial support from advertisers and to briefly identify a donor's products and services.

Nielsen Media Research estimated that by the year 2003, 67.4 percent of homes across the United States were linked to nearly 10,000 cable systems. Although millions of viewers continue to rely solely on local TV stations, Nielsen also estimated that there were 72 million basic cable customers in the United States in 2002.

A typical cable system has the technical capacity to offer between 36 and 60 channels or more of news, music, sports, movies, comedy, shopping, weather, and dozens of other programs. Some cable systems can offer more than one hundred channels.

Cable systems can also provide customers with other telecommunications services such as high-speed Internet access and local phone service. Using a cable modem allows Web users to surf the Internet at speeds much faster than those offered by dial-up services.

At least 5,300 cable systems originate local programs and maintain local access channels for community members to perform, voice opinions, or present public service messages. One quarter of all cable systems solicit and air local advertising. Pay-per-view movies are available on cable systems in every state.

This expansion of digital-based technology has generated billions of dollars for TV, radio, cable, hardware and software manufacturers, and thousands of related businesses. It also has created many exciting new jobs, which should come as welcome news for young people who are training for a career in electronic communications.

New Media Era

Never before have people had such easy access to information or so many simple ways to communicate. Every day millions of people use digital technology to communicate locally, nationally, and internationally. Digital technology's ubiquity and ease of use has simplified the communication process and broadened the playing field for broadcast amateurs and professionals alike.

Relatively speaking, assimilation of digital technologies that replace analog systems has occurred rapidly and smoothly. Whereas it took most of the twentieth century to create radio, television, and cable infrastructure, twenty-first-century networks such as satellite systems, fiber optic cable networks, and wireless facilities are already off to a fast start. Chips on which digitized information is stored sell for a fraction of what they formerly cost, and computers, software, and modems are now more affordable than ever.

The multimedia explosion prompted Dietrich Ratzke, a prominent German journalist and educator, to suggest this analogy: "Had automobiles changed with the same speed as microelectronics, a mid-class car would today travel at one thousand kilometers per hour, would need only a liter of gas per thousand kilometers, would have enough room for one hundred passengers, and would cost about $10."

Electronic Narrowcasting

Broadcasters are less likely to target mass audiences than they once were, and a new policy of interactive narrowcasting to smaller audiences that share common interests has supplanted the traditional concept of broadcasting to the masses. Today broadcasters cater to small demographic clusters, taking aim at viewers and listeners with special interests.

Numerous Internet, radio, and cable TV programs are designed to appeal to particular economic, social, ethnic, and cultural groups. A typical radio station, for example, plays a particular style of music that appeals to a certain type of listener. Cable networks such as the Independent Film Channel, Oxygen, and Tech TV target specific viewers who have specialized interests.

This change came about because for many years, audiences were offered a limited menu of programs, personalities, and news services. Thanks to new technology and a boom in the number of audiovisual outlets and production houses, it is now possible in most communities to obtain entertainment and information from many different sources. Today viewers are no longer restricted in their program choices and are often faced with more options than they can handle.

Pay-per-view sports, movies, and special events constitute another form of narrowcasting. The same is true of armed forces radio and television stations, which are maintained all over the world for military personnel.

Many public and private institutions transmit programs from closed-circuit systems or low-power stations that they own. All such operations are designed to serve a relatively small number of people.

The Internet

In terms of narrowcasting diversity, no communications medium compares to the Internet. The World Wide Web has grown exponentially over the past several years and is now home to billions of websites that are dedicated to even the most obscure subject matter.

The importance of acquiring basic computer skills in today's high-tech world cannot be overstated. Never before have so many experienced the levels of interconnectivity or had access to the wealth of information now at their fingertips. A new generation of people is coming of age at a time of unprecedented technological advancement that has helped shape our culture. Many job opportunities are available for professionals who possess necessary computer skills, and those who do not are at a distinct disadvantage in many career fields.

In August 2000, the latest year for which figures are available, the U.S. Census Bureau found that some 54 million, or 51 percent, of households owned one or more computers. In addition, 44 million households included at least one member who used the Internet at home. This compares with the period between 1987 and 1997 in which the number of households with computers more than doubled, increasing from 18 percent to 40 percent. The number of Internet surfers grew at a comparable rate during that time.

Families that earned $75,000 per year or more were more likely to own a computer than lower-income households were. Among families in this earnings bracket, 88 percent owned at least one computer, and 79 percent included at least one family member who used the Internet at home. This compares with only 28 percent of households that earn $25,000 per year or less owning a computer.

Geographically, U.S. households in the West were more likely to own a computer than households in the South. Also, those living just outside large metropolitan areas were more likely to own a computer than those living in more rural areas.

Children are becoming especially adept at utilizing computers and the Internet. Census figures found that 94 million, or 36 percent, of people over the age of 3 used the Internet at home. That included 18 million young people between 3 and 17 years of age and 75 million young adults 18 years and older. In 1998 only 57 million people, or 22 percent, in the same age range used the Internet at home.

The U.S. Census Bureau found that e-mail was the most common Internet activity among adults and children. Among children who used the Internet at home, 73 percent used e-mail. Among adults, 88 percent used e-mail when online. Other popular uses included school research, job and information searches, news, shopping, and entertainment (see Table 1.1).

Electronic Communications

Everywhere you go technology has transformed a once-limited world of knowledge and awareness into an unlimited universe of sights and sounds. Turn on your TV set and right before your eyes,

Table 1.1 Specific Internet Uses at Home by Adults and Children, August 2000

Specific Use	Children 3 to 17	Adults 18 and Over
Any Internet use	18,437 (100%)	75,322 (100%)
E-mail	13,438 (72.9%)	66,046 (87.7%)
School research	12,560 (68.1%)	18,080 (24.0%)
Check news, weather, and sports	3,658 (19.8%)	39,528 (52.5%)
Phone calls	630 (3.4%)	4,831 (6.4%)
Information search	6,079 (33.0%)	34,358 (64.2 %)
Job search	418 (2.3%)	14,930 (19.8%)
Job-related tasks	272 (1.5%)	25,347 (33.7%)
Shop or pay bills	1,467 (8.0%)	30,014 (39.8%)
Play games, entertainment	1,981 (10.7%)	3,655 (4.9%)
Other	1,099 (6.0%)	7,051 (9.4%)

Source: U.S. Census Bureau

satellite delivery systems give you a front-row seat and a close-up view of people making news all over the globe and in the outer reaches of space. Flip a switch on a computer and you have access to vast amounts of information, entertainment, and services.

It is not surprising why so many young people are attracted to broadcasting. They envision a unique opportunity to work in an exciting, ever-changing environment and to engage in humanity's oldest, and perhaps its most important, activity—the art of communication.

Immediacy in communications is an important consideration in virtually everything we do, and we are expected to respond quickly to every situation. Businesses place a premium on immediacy as billions of e-mails transmitting documents and information fly all over the world each day at lightning speeds. Cell phones enable friends, families, and coworkers to connect with one another via voice or text anywhere, anytime. Text messaging has spawned a new shorthand language that many young people have adopted and would say is "E-Z 4 U 2 Use."

Modern methods of communication strongly influence our lifestyles, our thinking, and our values. We depend on electronic media for information, enlightenment, advertising, and entertainment. They answer our need for companionship, counseling, spiritual support, and babysitting. But the arteries of communication have multiplied and changed as merging technologies have given birth to countless new websites, cable channels, networks, and various kinds of interactive facilities.

Although these new avenues of communication caused some job loss in traditional media, they should produce a sizable number of fresh employment opportunities in an expanding multimedia marketplace.

Employment Outlook

If you choose to pursue a career in broadcasting, keep in mind the importance of the endeavor and approach the task with respect and enthusiasm. You will be joining a profession with great social, cultural, and commercial responsibilities. Don't pursue a broadcasting career unless you intend to become a trustworthy communicator.

Whether you are self-employed or working for a public or private organization, competitive pressures will dictate that you are equipped—mentally, physically, and emotionally—and that you remain focused on your career objectives. Success and contentment won't come only from the money you make or a lofty job title, but from providing a service that is helpful to others and satisfying to you.

Because many employers have placed greater responsibilities upon fewer people, it's advisable to be multitalented and technically proficient. Most broadcasting employees are required to be versatile professionals who are capable of working in more than one area. A small video production firm may have one employee who acts as scriptwriter, announcer, and producer. A radio announcer also may be assigned news, music, and engineering duties.

If you seek employment in the rapidly evolving digital technology industry, you will have many options. But to qualify for them you will have to be well educated, both academically and technically, so be prepared to study and utilize the latest technology. Keep in mind that you are learning to be a multimedia expert who is technically, culturally, and socially proficient in responding to the needs and preferences of a discriminating public. If you apply yourself to this task with adequate knowledge and the right attitude, you will find success.

While technical skills will improve your chances of finding and holding on to a good job, getting promoted demands ingenuity and resourcefulness. "The industry will pay and pay well for people who know how to implement tomorrow's technology to help their stations make money," says Brad Dick, editorial director of Broadcast Engineering. "If you're one of them, your future is bright."

Most jobs in TV, radio, cable, and related media require a college degree or some other form of higher education. Computer skills and knowledge of the various software programs that relate to your industry are of paramount importance. In addition, many employers also require a working knowledge of digital technology, communications skills, motivation, and a proven ability to work quickly and meet deadlines. You should try to become so reliable and efficient that you will be able to make a comfortable living under constantly changing—and sometimes adverse—conditions.

The proliferation of cable channels has created a need for additional people to write, produce, and market programs. The Internet has generated similar job opportunities as websites devoted to business and entertainment crop up daily. New media professionals who specialize in Web design are also in demand.

Jobs are plentiful for media professionals in advertising, public relations, video production, sales, marketing, promotion, and businesses that operate in-house or network communications systems. Schools and colleges are seeking qualified educators to teach communications courses and manage broadcasting facilities.

According to a survey conducted by the Radio-Television News Directors Association and Foundation (RTNDA) and Ball State University, data collected at the end of 2001 found that layoffs and hiring freezes caused employment within 733 local television news departments in the United States to decrease by 14.6 percent from the previous year. Independent stations dropped by 16 percent compared with a 12.5 percent decrease at network affiliates. Although the total number of radio news continued to decrease, staff sizes did not.

2

A History of the Field

As early as the 1860s, a physicist in Scotland named James Clerk Maxwell spent long hours in his laboratory trying to determine whether radio waves existed and could be used for communication. Finally, in 1888, a German physicist named Heinrich Rudolph Hertz confirmed that rapid variations of electric current could be projected into space in the form of radio waves that were similar to light and heat waves.

By the 1890s, wireless experiments were being carried out in France, Russia, Italy, Germany, England, and the United States. Most considered the tests to be nothing more than a fascinating novelty. But a growing number of scientists, military strategists, and business leaders were intrigued by what they heard and supported further research and development.

In 1895 an Italian engineer named Guglielmo Marconi capitalized on the accumulated findings by successfully sending and receiving radio signals over a short distance. A year later he obtained a British patent for his transmitting device. As the twentieth century dawned, he initiated transatlantic radio tests. Today Marconi is often referred to as the "Father of Broadcasting."

At the St. Louis World's Fair in 1904, one of the main attractions was a wireless tower operated by a young scientist named Lee De Forest. Three years later, he formed the De Forest Radio Telephone Company and began a prolonged series of experiments designed to convince the public that music and voices could be conveyed by radiotelephone.

On January 13, 1910, Enrico Caruso broadcast several songs from the stage of the Metropolitan Opera House in New York. The transmitting antenna was suspended from two fishing poles on the roof of the opera house as small groups of radio buffs in New York and New Jersey listened to the history-making concert.

In 1912 the U.S. Navy adopted the name *radiotelegraph* for its wireless operations. It later coined the term *broadcast* to refer to dissemination of orders to the fleet. By 1915 the Bell Telephone Company was broadcasting frequent voice tests from Arlington, Virginia, and receiving reception reports from all over the United States and several other countries.

Radio Growth and Regulation

The first radio licensing law in the United States was enacted in 1912. Although it was an inadequate answer to the needs of this rapidly growing medium, the legislation served for 15 years as the country's basic rules for radio operations.

The law authorized wavelengths and operational times to be assigned to applicants. Different spectrum positions were allotted to ships, governmental agencies, and amateurs. A provision was made for some experimental permits as well. Soon after the law went into effect, more than a thousand broadcasters applied for and received licenses. Hundreds of additional licenses were issued in the years that followed.

Initially, all broadcasting was noncommercial. But in 1919 some radiotelephone experimenters received permission to operate on a limited commercial basis.

Following the first National Radio Conference in 1922, a new AM transmitter was authorized for use and maximum power usage was increased to one thousand watts. Demand for licenses remained so strong that the standard broadcast band was increased from 550 kilocycles to 1,500 kilocycles, and transmitter power was upped again to five thousand watts.

As the number of AM radio stations multiplied, the air became cluttered with signals, causing serious interference problems. The situation went uncorrected because existing laws lacked enforcement provisions. Many broadcasters illegally changed frequencies, boosted power, and transmitted longer hours than authorized. At the Fourth National Radio Conference in 1925, concerned delegates appealed to the government to make radio stations play by the rules.

The Dill-White Radio Act of 1927 created a five-member Federal Radio Commission and empowered its members to issue licenses, allocate frequencies, and control transmitter wattage. The act designated the secretary of commerce to inspect radio stations, examine their methods of operation, and assign permanent call letters only to qualified licensees. It was a start in the right direction, but a more comprehensive law was not passed until seven years later.

The Communications Act of 1934

In 1933 President Franklin Delano Roosevelt requested that Secretary of Commerce Daniel C. Roper appoint an interdepartmental committee to study and deal with the nation's electronic communications needs and problems. The committee recommended that

Congress establish a single agency to regulate all interstate and foreign communication by wire and radio, which included telephone, telegraph, and broadcast. As a result, the Communications Act of 1934 was passed and the seven-member Federal Communications Commission (FCC) was created to administer the unified legislation.

The act incorporated some provisions from the earlier Radio Act, but added much-needed regulation and supervision measures. This is the statute under which the FCC has operated since July 11, 1934. The size of the commission, however, was reduced to five members in 1983.

Here are just a few ways in which the FCC regulates the broadcasting industry:

- Allocates space in the radio frequency spectrum to all broadcast services and to many auxiliary and nonbroadcast services that employ radio technology
- Assigns location, frequency, and power to stations in each service within the allocated frequency bands
- Regulates broadcasting by inspection of existing stations to ensure that they operate in accordance with FCC rules and technical provisions. Serious violations are subject to monetary fines and even revocation of license
- Assigns call letters, issues transmitter and operational licenses, and processes requests for transfer of license ownership. Also reviews each station's record at time of renewal to see if it is operating in the public interest

Development of Television

The history of television closely parallels that of radio because growth of the wireless movement intensified interest in transmitting sights as well as sounds. As early as 1884, a German scientist named Paul Nipkow developed a scanning device for sending pictures wirelessly. Three years later, another German named K. F. Braun invented the cathode ray tube.

In 1907 two scientists working independently of one another—A. A. Campbell-Swinton in England and Boris Rosing in Russia—almost simultaneously developed the basic principles of modern television. Four years later, Campbell-Swinton designed a television camera.

These and other pioneering efforts coalesced in the United States when a Russian immigrant named V. K. Zworykin applied in 1923 for a patent on the iconoscope camera tube.

By 1927 several U.S. broadcasting stations were experimenting with television. One program, transmitted by wire from Washington, D.C., to New York featured Herbert Hoover, who at the time served as secretary of commerce. RCA demonstrated large-screen TV in 1930 from RKO's Fifty-Eighth Street Theatre in Manhattan. In 1936 the British Broadcasting Corporation (BBC) introduced a public television service. Soon afterward, 17 experimental TV stations operated in the United States.

Franklin Roosevelt was the first president to be televised when he opened the New York World's Fair in 1939. That same year saw the first telecast of major league baseball, college football, and professional boxing. After World War II, television began to expand nationwide and became a major new entertainment and advertising medium.

Public Broadcasting

Although broadcasting in America is primarily a commercial system supported by revenues from advertisers, hundreds of noncommercial radio and television stations provide the public with educational and cultural programming.

The government initiated this type of broadcasting by issuing some of the first AM radio licenses to educational institutions. By 1925 more than 170 schools and colleges owned and operated their own stations. The FCC no longer grants permits for AM educational stations, and few remain on the air. But it continues to encourage public broadcasting by allocating FM and TV channels to noncommercial applicants.

Public broadcasting facilities are not required to stay on the air for any specified number of hours, but they are expected to ascertain and respond to educational and cultural needs of the communities they serve. Their daily programs are beamed to millions of students in classrooms and also are available to the general public.

The Corporation for Public Broadcasting is a nongovernmental statutory organization that was created to provide support and guidance to public radio and television stations. It receives both federal funding and private donations. Some of the money goes directly to individual stations, but most is used to subsidize programming for member stations of National Public Radio and Public Broadcasting Service.

National Public Radio (NPR) is a noncommercial, satellite-delivered radio system that provides some 540 FM stations with programs and promotional and fund-raising assistance. NPR also represents its member stations in Washington on issues affecting broadcasters.

Public Broadcasting Service (PBS) is a nonprofit corporation that supplies programming, research, and promotional assistance to most of the nation's public television stations. Numerous other TV shows are developed for PBS by regional networks and stations such as WGBH in Boston and WQRD in Pittsburgh.

Only a limited number of jobs exist at public TV and radio stations. Staffs are small and salaries are modest. But working conditions usually are favorable, and the pace generally is less stressful than in commercial operations. An added incentive is the opportunity to work in a field that is dedicated to education.

Public Radio International (PRI) acquires, develops, funds, and distributes radio programs via satellite to 540 public FM stations in the United States, Guam, and Puerto Rico. In cooperation with NPR and the Corporation for Public Broadcasting, PRI serves all of Europe with 24-hour English-language programming. PRI also cooperates with the BBC and WGBH in Boston to produce "The World," a weekly radio news magazine aired in Europe and the United States.

The following are other types of public broadcasting stations to consider:

- **Campus radio stations.** In 1948 the FCC authorized schools to obtain broadcast licenses for 10-watt FM-educational stations. With low-powered equipment that is easy to install and simple to operate, this type station transmits a weak signal to a limited campus area.
- **College carrier-current radio.** Some schools and colleges have small radio stations that transmit their programming by carrier current. Reception is confined to on-campus listening. This kind of station does not require FCC registration, but it can provide practical experience for student broadcasters.
- **Closed-circuit TV and radio.** Many schools have closed-circuit systems linking classrooms for instructional purposes. This service is transmitted by cable. Since no actual broadcast is involved, such operations are not subject to government regulation.
- **Satellite Education Resources Consortium (SERC).** This organization of educators and public broadcasting systems in more than 20 states is a cooperative venture for developing

and delivering instructional resources to students and teachers. One such method, interactive television, permits students at home or in a classroom to see and converse with an instructor in a remote studio. A number of state school systems use this methodology to teach courses in math, science, and foreign languages.

Licensed and Unlicensed Low-Power Narrowcasting

The FCC issues licenses for several low-power AM, FM, and TV operations. The limits on power and coverage radius are 250 watts and 25 miles for AM, and 100 watts and 4 miles for both FM and TV. Stations may be either commercial or noncommercial but transmit only educational or informational messages.

Some air weather reports, travel advisories, and promotional announcements for parks, museums, or tourist attractions. Others serve as mobile relay stations, supply public safety and special emergency radio services, or supply industrial and land transportation radio services. These low-power outlets narrowcast to a small, specific type of audience.

The FCC permits the manufacture and operation of small AM and FM transmitters that generate a maximum effective radiated power of .01 microwatts. They are designed to blanket a coverage radius of only two hundred to three hundred feet. No license is required, and there are no restrictions on hours of operation.

A typical transmitter weighs only two and a half pounds and functions automatically with an audiocassette or digital chip mechanism. Schools and churches use such facilities to communicate with their respective audiences. Banks and real estate firms and fast-food restaurants rely on these miniature transmitters for sales and marketing purposes. Some residential neighborhoods operate their own low-power radio bulletin board. FCC rules do not permit unlicensed stations of this kind to be heard on television broadcast bands.

The Telecommunications Act of 1996

When the Telecommunications Act of 1996 was finally passed after spending 12 years in Congress, its advocates hailed the landmark act, saying it would create a multitude of jobs, encourage diversity of voices and viewpoints, foster competition, and usher in a new information age. To do this, Congress mandated that large telephone carriers that previously held a monopoly in the local market make their networks available to competitive carriers.

But the act triggered a flurry of buyouts and corporate mergers. It also has intensified rivalry among phone companies, cable system operators, and other local and long-distance communications systems.

The Telecommunications Act of 1996 removed all restrictions on the number of AM and FM radio stations that one company can own but limited ownership in individual markets as follows: a maximum of eight radio properties in markets with more than 45 stations; up to seven in markets with 30 to 44 stations; as many as six in markets with 15 to 29 stations; and a maximum of five in markets with fewer than 15 stations.

Rules regarding television also have been relaxed to permit a company to own an unlimited number of TV stations nationwide, provided their combined reach does not exceed 35 percent of the country's television audience. However, the rule limiting ownership to one TV station per market remains unchanged.

Other provisions of the Telecommunications Act of 1996 include:

- Permits common ownership of cable systems and broadcast networks
- Extends the license terms of TV and radio stations to eight years
- Immediately ends rate regulation of smaller cable systems and provides for eventual rate deregulation of larger systems
- Allows TV networks to start and own an additional broadcast network
- Requires new TV sets to come equipped with a V-chip for screening out objectionable programming
- Imposes fines for transmission of pornography on the Internet

Broadcast Law and Policy

The FCC ordinarily does not prescribe the content or amount of subject matter to be broadcast. Individual radio and TV stations decide on the nature of their programming and select everything they broadcast, including entertainment, news, sports, public affairs, commercials, and other subjects. Each licensee is expected to continually ascertain the needs and interests of the people in its coverage area and to respond with appropriate programming. The commission does require, however, that television stations air at least three hours of shows each week for children.

Although the FCC is forbidden to exercise broadcast censorship, it can prohibit transmission of false, obscene, or fraudulent information. Unless material represents a "clear and present danger of serious substantive evil," it is protected as free speech under the First Amendment. The FCC can, however, restrict material it deems indecent if there is a risk that the audience may include children. To that end, the commission prohibits indecent television and radio shows to air between 6:00 A.M. and 10:00 P.M.

Obscene material, on the other hand, is not guaranteed First Amendment protection and cannot be broadcast. Although obscene material is open to subjective interpretation, the FCC says that for material to be considered obscene, it must meet the following criteria:

- An average person, applying contemporary community standards, must find that the material, as a whole, appeals to the prurient (arousing lustful feelings) interest.
- The material must depict or describe, in a patently offensive way, sexual conduct specifically defined by applicable law.
- The material, taken as a whole, must lack serious literary, artistic, political, or scientific value.

Penalties for violations range from reprimands and cease-and-desist orders to fines. If an offense is extremely serious, the FCC can revoke a license or deny its renewal.

In 2001 the FCC reviewed its Broadcast-Newspaper Cross-Ownership Rule and Local Radio Ownership Rule. In September 2002 the commission reviewed its four other broadcast ownership rules: Television-Radio Cross-Ownership, Dual Network, Local Television Ownership, and National Television Ownership.

The FCC formed the Media Ownership Working Group at the end of 2001 as a first step toward developing a foundation for reevaluating FCC media ownership policies designed to promote competition, diversity, and localism in the media market.

3

BROADCASTING CAREER FIELDS

EMPLOYMENT OPPORTUNITIES FOR broadcasters are expected to increase over the next several years, but growth will vary throughout different areas of the industry.

Thousands of trained broadcasters find jobs with public and private organizations where they work as advertising professionals, salespeople, marketing and promotion managers, public relations and public information officers, and directors of development. One of the best job markets for electronic communicators exists in the retail business community, where many firms conduct intensive radio and TV advertising, marketing, and sales promotion. Applicants for these positions should have strong written, verbal, and technical skills.

Armed with a degree in journalism and some professional experience, you should find a good job with any number of organizations including major publications, online editions of newspapers, national and regional cable networks, professional associations and societies, syndicated news services, advertising agencies, video and production studios, colleges and universities, or research firms.

The following are brief descriptions of the various career paths within this exciting field. We'll explore each section in greater detail throughout the book.

Announcers

Landing an announcer job in radio and television will remain highly competitive as the number of job seekers outweighs available jobs. The pay is generally low for beginners, and applicants will have a better chance of being hired at a small radio station. Those seeking work in a large market typically must show they can attract and retain a large audience.

Those in this position announce program information and station breaks; read news, weather, traffic, and public service announcements; research and write scripts; play music selections; take phone calls from listeners; interview guests; and make public appearances. Many announcers begin in unrelated positions such as production assistant, camera operator, or reporter and move into an on-air position later in their careers.

In 2002 there were 76,000 people in announcer jobs who earned between $6.14 and $24.92 per hour in the radio and television industry. Median pay for announcers in 2002 was $9.91 per hour.

Because new radio and television station development is expected to decline in coming years, the number of announcer jobs is expected to drop off through 2012. Also contributing to this decline will be alternative media sources such as the Internet, radio and television station consolidation, and technological advances.

Those seeking employment as an announcer at a television or radio station should have a college degree in broadcasting or technical school training in the field. High school and college students are encouraged to take courses in public speaking, drama, computer science, and other related activities. Gaining experience at a campus television or radio station is also valuable.

News Analysts, Reporters, and Correspondents

There were nearly 66,000 employees working as news analysts, reporters, and correspondents in 2002. Half of these worked at newspapers of varying sizes across the United States. The radio and television industry employed 25 percent of these workers, while the remaining percentage worked at magazines, wire services, and other media outlets. About four thousand of the total number of news analysts, reporters, and correspondents worked on a freelance basis.

By and large, available positions in these areas are expected to grow more slowly than in other industries through the year 2012. Mergers, consolidations, a decrease in advertising revenues, and a decline in the number of subscribers are all contributing factors to this downward trend. More rapid growth, however, is expected in radio, television, and at online versions of newspapers and magazines.

Landing a position with a large market newspaper, television station, or national consumer magazine will remain competitive, especially for recent college graduates. Although the pay is usually low, it will be easier for those getting started in communications to find a job with a small, regional newspaper or broadcast facility. Large-market newspapers and broadcast stations usually require three to five years' experience for employment consideration.

Although employers prefer a degree in journalism, other academic majors are considered as well. More than four hundred colleges and universities in the United States offer bachelor's degree programs in journalism. Course work can include media law and ethics, introductory mass media, reporting, writing, copyediting, television and radio newscasting, broadcast production, and various liberal arts subjects such as political science, psychology, history, and economics. Relevant internships or experience with a campus newspaper, television station, or radio station will also make candidates more attractive to employers.

Computer skills are particularly important for these media positions. Those interested in working at online versions of newspapers and magazines must be versed in the software required to combine text, audio, and video for stories that appear on the Web. Print journalists should also learn computer-assisted reporting skills, which allow journalists to access, compare, and analyze database information for use in articles.

With the exception of small newspapers or radio stations, salaries tend to be high but vary widely. The median annual salary for news analysts, reporters, and correspondents in 2002 was $33,320 for television and radio broadcasters and $29,090 at newspapers. The lowest 10 percent earned less than $17,620 per year, while the highest 10 percent earned more than $69,450.

Writers and Editors

Employment opportunities for writers and editors are expected to increase at about the same rate as other industries through 2012. Demand for more print and online publications, an increased number of retirees, and those leaving the industries to pursue other job opportunities will necessitate an increase in the number of workers needed to produce these materials.

Competition for these positions will be high, but low-paying jobs at small newspapers, radio stations, and television stations will be easier for beginners to find. Those getting started can expect to have responsibilities that include conducting research, copyediting, fact-checking other writers' work, and some writing. Technical writers who specialize in a given field such as engineering, law, or health care will have a better chance of obtaining higher-paying positions.

In 2002 about 319,000 writers and editors worked in the United States. Writers and authors represented 139,000 jobs, technical writers made up another 57,000, and 130,000 were in editing positions. One-half of all writer and editor jobs were salaried positions at newspapers, magazines, book publishers, and other information-related outlets.

Jobs at newspapers, trade magazines, and business journals were scattered across the country in 2002, but book publishing jobs were concentrated in major markets such as New York, Chicago, Boston, Los Angeles, Philadelphia, and San Francisco.

The median annual salary for writers and authors in 2002 was $42,790 overall and $33,550 at newspapers, periodicals, books, and directory publishers. Technical writers earned, on average, $50,580 in that same year. Median salaries for editors in 2002 were $41,170, with the lowest 10 percent earning less than $24,010 and the highest 10 percent earning more than $76,620.

A college degree is typically required for writing and editing positions. Although many employers will consider a broad-based liberal arts degree, most prefer those who have a degree in communications, journalism, or English. Employers also favor those who have worked for their high school or college newspaper, radio station, or television station.

Desktop Publishers

People in this position use computer software programs to combine visual elements such as photographs, graphs, and text into a finished product that is ready for publication in print or on the Web.

Computer technology advances in typesetting and page layout and design have simplified desktop publishing greatly, and positions in the field will grow faster than average through 2012.

Desktop publishers help create books, business cards, magazines, newspapers, and other materials. Pages are created entirely on a computer and appear on-screen as they will once they are printed.

A degree in graphic arts is one route that would-be desktop publishers can take, but other options are available. Many certificate programs and associate degree opportunities are available to those interested in learning the various software programs and design techniques required for a job in the field.

Depending on the size of the company and geographic area, annual salaries in 2002 ranged from $18,670 to more than $50,000. Positions are available across the United States, but more opportunities are available in large metropolitan areas. The median annual salary at commercial printing organizations in 2002 was $35,140 and $28,050 at newspapers.

Television, Video, and Motion Picture Camera Operators

Positions such as these require a blend of technical expertise, steady hands, and a creative eye. Camera operators record action and have knowledge of lighting and shot composition. Also called videographers or cinematographers, these professionals sometimes produce and edit the footage they shoot.

Camera operators shoot a variety of subjects and events including news, sports, motion pictures, music videos, documentaries, and private ceremonies. Many camera operators work at independent television stations, production houses, and cable outlets of varying sizes.

There were about 28,000 camera operators employed in the United States in 2002. About 20 percent of these were self-employed contract workers who were paid a daily rate or predetermined sum. In addition to technical and creative talents, freelance camera operators must also learn to write contracts, obtain permission for on-location shoots, secure copyright protection, and maintain detailed financial records. Freelancers purchase and own their equipment, which results in considerable expense.

The number of jobs available for camera operators is expected to increase at the same rate as other industries through 2012. But competition for these jobs will be tough given that many are attracted to the field. The median annual salary for camera operators in 2002 was $32,720. Those in the motion picture industry earned a median salary of $41,440, while those working in radio and television broadcasting earned $25,830.

Systems Analysts, Computer Scientists, and Database Administrators

Computers are at the core of the multimedia and information technology explosion, and those with the ability to maintain and develop hardware and software are in high demand. As computer systems technology continues to expand, job opportunities for systems analysts, computer scientists, and database administrators are expected to grow just as rapidly.

The growth of the Internet has also contributed to an increase in the number of computer-related positions, as specialists in website design, development, and maintenance are needed.

In 2002 there were 979,000 professionals working in various computer-related jobs, 89,000 of which were self-employed. Workers were distributed across the industry as follows: computer systems analysts—468,000; network systems and data communications analysts—186,000; database administrators—110,000; computer and information scientists in research—23,000; all other computer specialists—192,000.

Computer specialists come from many different backgrounds, and there is no specific way in which an employee should be trained. A college degree or a two-year associate's degree in computer science is generally acceptable. Graduate degrees are preferred. In addition to higher education, employers also emphasize prior experience and a demonstrated aptitude for computer systems maintenance.

Job opportunities for systems analysts, computer scientists, and database administrators are expected to increase rapidly through 2012. The median annual salary for network systems and data communications analysts was $58,420 in 2002. In the same year, computer and information scientists earned a median salary of $77,760. All other computer specialists earned a median salary of $54,070.

Broadcast and Sound Engineering Technicians and Radio Operators

These professionals install, maintain, and operate the electronic equipment—such as cameras, microphones, tape recorders, transmitters, and antennas—that the television, radio, cable, and motion picture industries use to record and transmit programs. Some find work in motion pictures, while others operate the soundboard at live music performances or act as sound engineers in a recording studio.

Competition for highly paid positions will be strong, and television stations will have more jobs available than radio stations. In 2002, of the 93,000 broadcast and sound engineering technicians and radio operators employed in the United States, one in three worked at a television or radio station.

Although jobs in television could be found across the country in 2002, employment opportunities with radio stations tended to be in smaller towns. The highest-paying jobs in radio and television were typically concentrated in large metropolitan areas such as New York City, Los Angeles, Chicago, and Washington, D.C.

The median annual salary for broadcast technicians in 2002 was $27,760. Sound engineers earned $36,970, and audio and video equipment operators earned a median salary of $31,110. Radio operators in 2002 had median annual earnings of $31,530.

Training in this field can be found at a number of universities, community colleges, and technical trade schools. Most beginners start at small television or radio stations before moving on to larger markets. In the motion picture industry, beginners gain experience working as editorial assistants under more experienced professionals.

Job growth through 2012 is expected be comparable to many industries. Although more technicians will be needed to meet the increased programming hours, television and radio broadcasting jobs are expected to decline due to increased use of computer-operated equipment. Cable industry employment is expected to increase rapidly as products such as cable modems and digital set-top boxes continue to hit the market.

4

TELEVISION IN THE UNITED STATES

TELEVISION PLAYS MANY roles in the lives of the American people. It can entertain, inform, or enrich one's life, or it can simply help kill time. Research indicates that a high percentage of viewers look to TV every day to provide news and information, entertainment, and education. A survey conducted by the Radio-Television News Directors Association and Foundation (RTNDA) and Bob Papper of Ball State University found that 81.4 percent of the U.S. population receives its news from local and network television coverage.

Congress and the Federal Communications Commission (FCC) have authorized some two thousand television channels to operate in communities throughout the United States. The country is divided into three geographical zones, each of which is permitted a certain number of VHF and UHF channels. The channel number and zone of a station determine its maximum power, antenna height, and the distance it must be from other stations on the same channel.

Although commercial TV stations are required to broadcast at least 28 hours per week, most remain on the air for longer periods of time. Many operate 24 hours a day, seven days a week. Some TV outlets use low-power translators and boosters to carry their signal into hard-to-reach areas. TV stations also reach additional viewers via cable systems and websites.

The majority of television stations are affiliated with major networks such as ABC, CBS, NBC, and Fox. An affiliate usually carries at least three hours of network programs at night and some daytime shows. Stations obtain additional programs from networks and syndication companies that specialize in the sale and distribution of news, weather, sports, music, comedy, movies, cultural programs, and special events.

Congress has required that TV stations must convert from analog to digital broadcasting systems by December 31, 2006. To provide a smooth transition to digital television (DTV), the FCC has adopted so-called "plug and play" rules that will ensure that most cable systems are compatible with DTV receivers, as well as other electronic equipment.

As of May 2003, at least one digital station served every major television market, and more than 1,000 DTV stations were on the air. Stations are required to broadcast in both analog and digital formats until the transition is complete.

A television station that is not affiliated with a network is commonly referred to as an independent. Instead of relying on a network to supply much of its news and programming, the independent outlet develops many of its own productions and purchases or leases programs from outside sources.

Independents typically rely on motion pictures and reruns of television shows previously shown on network-affiliated stations. Some independents narrowcast by specializing in one type of video, such as religion, news, sports, or talk.

Since it produces and markets many of its own programs, a well-run independent station can be a busy and stimulating place to work. Opportunities to handle various assignments allow employees at independent stations to receive a fuller experience than they could obtain at a network affiliate.

Jobs in Marketing, Promotion, and Research

Marketing, promotion, and research is a dynamic area of television that would best be suited for those who like to work in a fast-paced, constantly evolving field. In this area, you'll need to have knowledge of market trends, demographics, and a keen sense of what the competition is doing. If this sounds exciting and challenging, the following career paths in this field may be the perfect choice for you.

Marketing Manager

This marketing professional is responsible for developing strategic concepts and tailoring campaigns to increase the revenue, popularity, and prestige of a television station. The work entails initiating research projects and analyzing the results to determine the needs of advertisers and viewers, and then devising innovative ways in which to satisfy those needs by mobilizing the television station's sales, programming, and promotional resources.

Promotion Director

Often known as director of creative services, this person is responsible for promoting the television station's image, programs, and personalities through advertising, publicity, promotion, and public relations. A major duty is producing in-house promotional spots with computer graphics. This department also prepares and distributes press releases, program schedules, promotional brochures, and pamphlets. It may also develop contests, special events, and public relations projects.

The job requires a college degree plus experience in broadcasting, advertising, or public relations. Since media buying and other expense-related duties are involved, knowledge of accounting and budgeting is an asset.

Promotion Assistant

A promotion assistant works under the supervision of the promotion director. The job demands creative promotional skills and a mastery of computer graphics software. A promotion assistant helps develop various promotional concepts used to promote a station's image. Prerequisites are a degree in broadcasting or advertising and some TV experience. Average base pay for all markets is about $20,000 to $25,000.

Research Director

This person collects data and interprets research studies to help management make programming, sales, and marketing decisions. To prepare for this job, you need a college degree with knowledge of computer research methodology, statistics, marketing, economics, and broadcasting. Average salary is about $45,000. Small stations pay less. Large stations pay up to $75,000 or more.

TV stations that do not have a research director contract for such services when needed or request assistance from the research departments of their national sales representatives.

Sales Positions

Television is a complex and dynamic business that depends heavily on research, demographics, psychographics, and sophisticated marketing to satisfy the demands of advertisers. Unlike newspapers, magazines, and pay-TV, which collect subscriber fees, commercial television stations derive their revenue primarily from the sale of spot announcements and program sponsorships to local, regional, and national advertisers.

The amount and percentage of income derived from each source varies considerably. For example, national advertisers spend far more money in large markets than they do in small ones. In addition to their own sales staffs, most television stations employ a national sales representative firm that has office locations in principal cities to reach and sell major advertisers throughout the country. The following are descriptions of various sales positions.

General Sales Manager

This person heads the television station's sales team. He or she is the person responsible for preparing sales forecasts and directs local and national sales efforts to meet budget projections in advertising sales. Job requirements are a business or broadcasting degree, five or more years of television sales experience and expertise in marketing, research, pricing, inventory control, finance, and personnel management. Average base pay is about $90,000, but additional compensation can increase the total annual salary to $130,000 or more.

National Sales Manager/Assistant Sales Manager

The national or assistant sales manager is responsible for selling and servicing advertising accounts located beyond the TV station's primary coverage area. He or she works closely with national sales representatives and functions as assistant to the general sales manager in some operations. Candidates should have a college degree, a minimum of three years in broadcast sales, and knowledge of marketing, research, and computers. Compensation is likely to be salary plus a percentage of the national advertising revenue.

Local Sales Manager

The local sales manager recruits, trains, and supervises a staff of local salespeople. He or she assigns accounts and checks reports of contacts made and results obtained. The job also entails working with the general sales manager and marketing and research directors to develop new business and increase the size of existing accounts. Prior success as a salesperson and demonstrated management and marketing skills will help qualify you for this job. You should have a college education and several years of impressive performance in sales and marketing.

Account Executive

This job is involved with selling and marketing programs to local retail and corporate advertisers. An account executive must have good written and oral presentation skills, the ability to interpret research findings, and the ability to promote support services provided by the station. Applicants to these positions should also be able to develop and retain accounts. Computer skills and a college degree are preferred. Annual compensation includes salary plus commission and averages about $60,000. Some can earn twice that amount.

Sales Service Coordinator

This administrative assistant to the general sales manager collects, collates, and distributes TV sales information, manages sales data, prepares sales research materials, and expedites trade agreements. The sales service coordinator also trains and supervises sales department assistants. A college degree is preferred. Computer experience and a good record in business management are essential. Annual earnings average $45,000 in salary plus $10,000 in other compensation.

Traffic Manager

The traffic manager is responsible for setting up and maintaining scheduling instructions and timings for all commercial accounts, programs, and promotional and public service announcements. He or she assembles and processes the data needed to produce the daily operational schedule.

The job requires computer skills, attention to detail, and accuracy. College training is desirable, plus experience as a traffic assistant.

Sales Order Processor

This person collects, verifies, and records every advertising order received at the television station. He or she checks for accuracy and completeness of instructions. The sales order processor also may assist in preparation of sales and inventory reports.

Minimal job requirements are a high school diploma and computer skills. Experience using spreadsheet programs such as Microsoft Excel is a plus. Business training and broadcast experience is also helpful.

Management and Administrative Jobs

The following jobs are for those who like to run a tight ship, can make sure that all players on the team have everything they need to do their job well, and are comfortable making difficult decisions and providing guidance. Persons best suited to this area are also comfortable with new technologies and have exceptional organizational and communications skills. The following are descriptions of a variety of managerial positions within broadcasting.

General Manager

Intense competition, changing technology, and rising costs forced television mangers to become more involved in the day-to-day operations of their stations. Together with department heads, the general manager makes decisions regarding programming, sales, hiring of personalities, and contracting for special events and promotions. Turning a profit is so crucial that TV managers rely heavily on the advice of research, marketing, technical, and financial experts in making both short-term and long-term commitments.

To qualify for this position you should have a successful record of 10 years or more in broadcast sales, programming, and management. Compensation may be a straight salary or salary and bonus, depending on station performance. National average earnings are $190,000.

Station Manager

Duties and responsibilities of this second-in-command position reflect the wishes of the general manager. Although qualifications for the job are similar to those of the general manager, compensation is less, averaging $105,000.

Operations Manager

Supervision of production and technical operations at the TV station is the daily responsibility of this official. The job requires technical and managerial capabilities. You should have a communications degree and considerable broadcast experience. Some TV news departments have their own operations managers. Salaries range from $45,000 to $85,000. The national average is $60,000.

Business Manager

This financial officer manages accounting policies and procedures; develops financial data for budgets, reports, and projections; supervises accounting employees; and serves as financial consultant to all department heads. Duties may include purchase and maintenance of nontechnical equipment and supplies. The position requires a business degree and accounting experience.

Accountant

An accountant assists the business manager in running the financial operations of the television station. He or she handles accounts receivable and payable, billings, and payroll. The job also includes maintaining financial records for use by management in daily business dealings and budgeting. Prerequisites are business school training, knowledge of accounting software programs, accuracy with numbers, and an analytical mind.

Human Resource Manager

This person is responsible for recruiting job applicants and supplying department heads with the names and résumés of prospective employees. The manager of human resources maintains records of all station employees and prepares required reports for management and the government. He or she communicates with employees regarding station policies and encourages activities to promote morale within the organization. A college degree is preferred, with training and experience in personnel management.

Engineering Careers

Most stations operate with fewer technicians than they once did. Yet stations require more and different engineering expertise than ever before because of technological and marketplace changes.

Rapid and steady development of sophisticated communications equipment demands that technicians continue to learn about new devices and how best to use them. Expensive, intricate electronic components also require careful maintenance. Now more than ever, engineering personnel are expected to combine technical knowledge with a sharp sense of showmanship and budget-mindedness.

Prerequisites for employment are a college degree, technical training, prior experience at a radio station or smaller TV station, and an aptitude for operations or maintenance.

Technical Director

This specialist is responsible for the technical quality of a television production and supervises the technical crew. The technical director transmits instructions from the producer to camera operators and sound and lighting technicians. The job also involves operating video switching equipment. It requires a combination of technical know-how and creative production talents. Salary range is $21,000 to $37,000. The average for all markets is $29,000.

Audio Operator

The audio operator is responsible for the audio portion of a television program, controls switching of microphones, and monitors sound levels on voices, music, and special effects.

Video Operator

The video operator is responsible for the television picture, performs the necessary functions to control brightness and color levels, and monitors transmission of the video signal to the transmitter.

Camera Operator

This person operates both full-sized studio cameras and smaller electronic news gathering (ENG) cameras inside a studio or on location, and focuses on the action as directed by the producer/director. Some TV stations and network news programs have replaced camera operators with computer-controlled robotic cameras.

Film Operator

This person is responsible for operating the recording, playback, and editing functions at a TV station. On the producer/director's request, he or she cues up and projects tapes, films, cassettes, or slides.

Maintenance Technician

Maintenance technicians are responsible for the repair and servicing of a TV station's communications equipment and facilities. Each technician usually is assigned one area of maintenance responsibility, such as the transmitter, ENG cameras, studio cameras, or satellite facilities.

Network Television Jobs

Network television jobs are similar in most respects to those found at non-network stations. People work in programming, sales, news, engineering, promotion, public relations, research, human resources, and general administration. In addition, networks have legal and affiliate-relations departments. When hiring performers, networks usually prefer those with considerable experience and impressive credentials. Individuals already on staff often fill these openings. Some network salaries—especially those of news anchors—are high, but compensation for most positions is about the same as at large TV stations.

5

CABLE TELEVISION

BEFORE CABLE TELEVISION blanketed the country, most viewers in the United States could only watch the network offerings aired by local VHF and UHF stations. Now cable and satellite systems have vastly increased the available choices.

Cable and Satellite Systems

According to the National Cable and Telecommunications Association (NCTA), more than two hundred cable networks narrowcast various types of specialized programming. The Discovery Channel, USA Network, CNN, ESPN, and numerous other networks air news, sports, movies, and original programming to millions of subscribers. In 2003, TBS Superstation was credited with having the most subscribers—nearly 88 million.

The U.S. cable industry shows continued growth and has added new subscribers each year since 1980. According to Nielsen Media Research, there were 17.7 million basic customers in 1980, which

Table 5.1 Cable Industry Overview

Basic Cable Customers (November 2003)	73,365,880
U.S. Television Households (January 2004)	108,410,160
Cable Penetration of TV Households (December 2003)	67.7%
Occupied Homes Passed by Cable (December 2003)	95%
Basic Cable/Homes Passed (December 2003)	71.3%
Cable Headends (May 2003)	9,889
Premium Cable Units	50,614,000
Cable Systems	9,339
Cable Employees (1999)	130,953
Annual Cable Revenue (2003)	$51.3 billion
Total Advertising Revenue (2002)	$14.7 billion
Annual Franchise Fees Paid by Cable Industry (2003)	$2.4 billion
Digital Cable Customers (September 30, 2003)	21,500,000
Cable Modem Customers (September 30, 2003)	15,000,000
Homes Passed by Cable Modem Service (September 30, 2003)	90,000,000+

Source: All figures courtesy of the National Cable and Telecommunications Association

represented 22.6 percent of television households. By December 2003, the total number of subscribers had reached 73.4 million, representing 67.7 percent of U.S. households (see Table 5.1).

Premium cable channels such as HBO, Showtime, and Starz have also shown steady growth. Between 1983 and 2002, the number of premium cable subscribers increased from 26.4 million to 53.2 million.

In addition to traditional basic cable services, broadband deployment increased as well. In 2003 there were 21.5 million digital cable subscribers and some 15 million customers using cable modems. In 2000 there were just six million digital cable customers in the United States. According to The Yankee Group, nearly 23 million U.S. households received high-speed Internet access via DSL or cable modems in 2003.

The industry invested heavily in 2003, pumping more than $10.6 billion into system upgrades and construction. As a result of the cable industry's $75 billion total investment, by 2004 advanced digital services were available in 85 million U.S. homes.

More than two hundred satellite-fed networks provide programming for cable systems. Many of the most popular such as CNN, MSNBC, Fox News Channel, and C-SPAN are devoted to news and public affairs, broadcasting 24 hours a day, seven days a week to more than one hundred countries.

Cable systems maintain one or more public access channels where local groups and individuals create and produce their own entertainment and informational programs. Some systems sell classified ads and market language courses, educational classes, and video shopping services.

As innovations in digital and fiber optic technology have transformed the broadcasting industry, cable companies have benefited from their ability to provide more channels, sharper pictures, and movies on demand. Many also provide a number of broadband interactive services such as high-speed Internet that compete with telecommunications companies, direct broadcast satellite, and Internet service providers.

Multiple system operators (MSO) such as Comcast, Time-Warner Cable, Charter Communications, and Cox Communications own a number of cable systems and have invested billions of dollars in their systems. Some offer digital cable, local telephone, and high-speed Internet service, and for a select few companies the investment has paid off with millions of subscribers. As of June 2003, Comcast claimed 21.4 million subscribers—roughly 29 percent of the total market share and twice that of its nearest competitor, Time-Warner Cable.

The following are brief descriptions of the various cable systems.

Pay Cable

This offers subscribers channels of special programming for which they pay a certain amount above the basic monthly charges. Home Box Office (HBO) initiated the first national interconnected pay network in 1975. In addition to contracting for program services of this type, many cable systems also lease channels to pay program operators or manage their own pay cable service and obtain programming from outside sources.

Pay-Per-View (PPV)

This is a method used by cable systems to market performances and events that would otherwise be seen only by those in attendance. Just as in-house cable systems in hotels offer feature films for a set fee, pay-per-view events are limited to spectators who pay for the privilege. To prevent people from watching without paying, programs are transmitted in scrambled signals that can be deciphered only by sets equipped with decoders.

Low-Power Television (LPTV)

Essentially television translator stations, these low-powered installations rebroadcast the signals of full-service stations and are used primarily to serve areas where normal TV reception is inadequate.

Multipoint Distribution Service (MDS)

This system uses microwaves to transmit video, data, text, or other services to customer-selected locations within a metropolitan area. Operators generally lease most of their time to pay-movie entrepreneurs who provide programming to hotels, apartment buildings, and homes.

Satellite Master Antenna Systems (SMATV)

Similar to cable systems, SMATV is not federally regulated and operates in limited areas. An earth station aimed at a cable satellite receives and transmits programming to individual apartment buildings, condominiums, or private housing developments.

Digital Television (DTV)

Digital TV delivers enhanced audio and video qualities and will replace analog systems by the end of 2006. Broadcasters can use digital television to offer viewers interactive and data services that are unavailable through analog systems.

High Definition Television (HDTV)

High definition TV is a form of digital television that offers a high-resolution picture quality and enhanced sound. Whereas conventional televisions provide 480 horizontal lines, a digital television picture is composed of 1,080 lines and offers much sharper image quality. HDTV also expands analog television's image ratio from 4:3 to 16:9, which means programs can be viewed in the same wide-screen format used in movie theaters.

In addition to superior video qualities, HDTV provides the same digital surround sound used in movie theaters and on DVDs.

Wireless Cable

Wireless cable transmits over microwave frequencies, and most systems offer 20 or more network channels to their customers. These channels are supplied through the combined facilities of multipoint distribution service (MDS), multichannel and multipoint distribution service (MMDS), instructional television fixed service (ITFS), and operational fixed service (OFS). In all, 33 channels are available, 20 of which come from ITFS and require transmitting five hours of educational programming per channel each week.

Digital Broadcast Satellite (DBS)

This video service bypasses networks, cable systems, and individual TV stations by transmitting from satellites stationed 22,300 miles above the earth to decoding disc antennas of individual subscribers. It only took four years for DBS systems to sign up six million customers. The business continues to grow as additional households contract for DBS delivery of 175 or more channels.

Some home satellite sets are equipped to receive even local TV stations, thereby eliminating the need to subscribe to a cable company for this service. Satellite companies are listed annually in the *Broadcasting and Cable Yearbook*, along with information about networks, common carriers, and program syndicators that use satellites to serve TV, radio, and cable operations. The federal government, phone companies, and international business firms are all big users of satellites.

Integrated Services Digital Network (ISDN)

Integrated Services Digital Network (ISDN) is a method of digital communication that allows you to talk, send and receive data, and transmit video and faxes over conventional phone lines. The digitized transmissions are reassembled at the other end of the line into high-quality images and sound.

Cable Network Jobs

Those who possess more than technical, programming, and production skills are more likely to be hired for the best-paying jobs in television. They understand the interrelationship of media and see the potential in new forms of electronic communications. Most important, they are helping their employers capitalize on the rapid growth of interactive technology.

According to the NCTA, in recent years cable systems have experienced growth in programming and production of local programs such as high school and college sports, town council meetings, and local talk shows. Cable networks have seen an increase in original programming that is produced in-house and purchased programming such as movies that ran in theaters.

The Federal Communications Commission estimated that in 1999, there were 130,953 cable industry employees who worked in a broad range of jobs across the cable industry. Cable systems, networks, and multiple system operators (MSO) need talented managers, technicians, legal specialists, and programming, sales, and marketing professionals to help the business run smoothly.

The following are descriptions of some cable network jobs.

President/CEO

This person is responsible for overseeing all of a cable network's departments and maximizing its number of subscribers and viewers. This requires day-to-day decisions regarding the network's programming, budgets, marketing efforts, and personnel. Qualifications usually include a college degree and several years of related management experience.

Programming Executive

This executive oversees the creation and coordination of a network's television show lineup. He or she develops programming budgets, purchases movies for networks to air, and works on program schedules.

Producer

The responsibilities of producers can include selecting casts, scheduling rehearsals, adapting scripts, overseeing camera staff, and deciding on camera angles. Producers can work on staff or be hired by a programming executive to oversee an in-house project. He or she discusses and approves budgets, scripts, talent, sets, props, lighting, and sound.

Account Executive

Generally speaking, account executives sell programming to cable system subscribers or sell cable advertising. Cable systems sometimes hire advertising majors and specialists in a particular sales field.

Regional Director

As part of the sales staff, the regional director oversees acquisitions.

VP Ad Sales

This executive is responsible for the network's advertising. Along with a support staff, the person in this position gears marketing efforts toward local businesses that speak to a particular demographic within the cable network's audience.

VP Affiliate Relations

This position represents a cable network by maintaining relationships with various affiliate stations.

Legal Affairs Representative

Cable networks are often involved in business dealings that involve contract drafting and negotiation. As a result, cable networks often hire experienced legal professionals to oversee these affairs.

Communications Director

This professional acts as a network's spokesperson. He or she is responsible for dealing with media inquiries, as well as contacting industry writers to communicate with the public via the press. Qualifications include a degree in communications, journalism, or public relations as well as experience in the field.

Personnel Director

This person is responsible for all aspects of employment including benefits, compensation, career development, and training.

VP Finance

The executive in this position oversees a cable network's financial health and budgets. He or she decides how much money a network is able to spend and where the money should be spent to best serve the network's goals.

Audio Technician

This person monitors sound levels and quality, adds sound effects, and oversees the music to be used in a broadcast.

Lighting Technician

This technician uses techniques such as shadow, highlights, and special lighting effects to create mood and enhance a production overall.

Floor Manager

This position is the link between the control room and the actors, technicians, and camera operators working on the set. The floor manager communicates direction from the control room to the floor and vice versa.

Editor

Once filming is complete, it is the editor's responsibility to work directly with the producer to cut the tape down to a more manageable size and connect the remaining pieces into a cohesive form.

Studio Technician

The studio technician manages all of a studio's technical aspects, repairing equipment and solving other technical problems that can arise.

Qualifications for the audio technician, lighting technician, floor manager, editor, and studio technician include a background in electronics and prior experience in the field.

Researcher

This person remains current on consumer trends by conducting studies and analyzing the results to gauge the likes and dislikes of audience segments. The results are used to determine how effective a particular program or promotion will be with a specific group of people or in a certain area.

Talent Booker

This position works with the researcher to determine who is best suited for a given production. He or she also works with talent agencies to discover new talent and contracts with existing celebrities.

Cable Systems Jobs

Cable systems hire a wide range of professionals to help deliver cable television to their customers. Although smaller systems may have one person work in a number of areas, a typical cable system employs staff to fill areas of management, technical, administrative, marketing, public relations, advertising, programming, and production. Among the most common job titles are the following:

General Manager

This executive oversees the entire cable system's operation and is responsible for hiring, directing, and consulting with department heads to develop strategies for growth and profitability. Pay varies according to the size of cable systems. The range is $60,000 to $275,000. Qualified individuals should have a degree in business and management experience in the industry.

Chief Engineer

The person in this job manages a team of skilled technicians who install, operate, and maintain a cable system's telecasting equipment. Responsibilities include cable-system design technical concepts, equipment planning, determining specification standards for equipment and materials, facility construction, equipment installation, and providing technical advice to other staff members.

A chief engineer should possess a high level of technical and managerial skill to balance and meet the needs of the system and personnel. This position requires a degree in engineering, broadcast experience, and technical, financial, and management expertise. Salaries range from $45,000 in small systems to $75,000 in large ones.

Trunk Technician

This employee repairs any electrical damage to a cable system's "trunk line," which is the main line that runs along major roads and into the system's plant. Damage to this line could cause a total system failure and it must be maintained.

Service Technician

The service technician makes service calls to the home to repair problems with a customer's cable service.

Bench Technician

This technician operates a system's repair facility where malfunctioning equipment is examined. He or she diagnoses any problems and completes the necessary repairs.

Installer

Cable installers prepare a subscriber's home for installation by connecting the appropriate wires and making the necessary adjustments to the customer's TV for cable reception.

Office Manager

This person heads the administrative staff and is responsible for overseeing daily business activities such as monitoring accounts receivable and payable, handling customer service complaints, and hiring and training staff. Qualified applicants should have prior experience in management or personnel.

Customer Service Representative

This employee deals directly with cable customers by phone or in person and tries to resolve problems and maintain customer satisfaction. College training in public relations and knowledge of cable system policies and programming are helpful in qualifying for this job. Pay ranges from $15,000 to $30,000.

Service Dispatcher

The person in this position fields calls from potential customers who want cable service and receives service interruption calls from existing customers. He or she then schedules appointments and communicates the service information to technicians.

Accounts Payable Clerk

This person works under the office manager and deals with the company's bills, deposits, purchase orders, and payroll.

Accounts Receivable Clerk

The accounts receivable clerk is responsible for maintaining customer payment records. When a customer is late with a payment, the accounts receivable clerk must take the appropriate measures to see that the company receives the money it is owed.

Billing Clerk

This employee must compute and distribute a detailed monthly bill that includes all of a subscriber's charges. Delinquent bills must be noted and dealt with accordingly.

Accountant

The accountant or bookkeeper oversees all of a cable system's budgets and financial matters. Primary responsibilities include maintaining accurate accounts payable and accounts receivable records and preparing monthly financial statements.

Public Affairs Director

This person acts as the go-between for a cable system and its local community. He or she meets with government officials, civic groups, and the local media to ensure that various community and governmental needs are met. Qualifications include a degree in marketing or public relations and experience in the field.

Marketing Director

This position works to increase a cable system's subscriber numbers through promotional programs, market research, and advertising.

Researcher

As part of the marketing department, a researcher conducts demographic studies and analyzes the results to determine the likes and dislikes of particular groups within the community. The aim is for the cable system to satisfy its customers by delivering the types of programs they want.

Sales Manager

This executive directs the cable system's sales staff and leads their efforts to add more subscribers and advertisers. College courses in marketing and professional experience in sales and advertising are assets in obtaining a cable sales position and later advancing to a management level, where salaries range from $35,000 to more than $50,000.

Director of Local Origination

This professional creates and coordinates community programming. He or she conceives programs, writes scripts, supervises production, manages staff, and plans budgets.

Director of Public Access

This position is responsible for overseeing cable channels that are available for public use. Although he or she may assist with and supervise programming, the cable system does not dictate programming produced for local access channels.

Director of Governmental or Educational Access

Much like the director of public access, this person oversees those in a community who want to use one of a cable system's local access channels to produce a governmental or educational program.

Multiple Systems Operators

Although some cable systems are individually owned, multiple systems operators (MSO) own and operate a number of different systems. Whereas a cable system strives to deliver quality cable service to its subscribers, MSOs provide support such as developing budgets and maintaining FCC records to their various cable outlets.

Employment within MSOs is almost identical to that of a cable system, but it adds another layer of corporate hierarchy that includes the following job titles: chairman, chief executive officer, chief operating officer, VP of corporate engineering, VP of operations management, VP of sales and marketing, VP of public affairs, VP of human resources, VP of finance, VP of legal affairs, director of research and development, director of MIS, director of training, regional manager, director of ad sales, director of telemarketing, director of marketing research, regional public affairs director, director of government affairs, director of personnel, director of accounting, and director of corporate development.

6

News Careers

Working for one of the news media today can be a fascinating and stimulating way to make a living. Here is a brief look at the environments and jobs available in television, radio, cable, and the Internet.

Television News

The average television station employs 35 to 40 news personnel and devotes most of its local program time to news, sports, weather, and hometown features. News staffs of 50 or more are common in large-city TV operations. Although one can certainly earn more money in another profession, thousands of young men and women choose to be television journalists.

Competition for TV news jobs is keen, and technical competence is stressed as a necessary qualification. Digital equipment is used for writing and editing copy and shooting video footage. Reporters carry electronic news gathering (ENG) cameras and

report from virtually any location. Versatility is a major consideration in hiring people for news jobs. Applicants are judged on their
ability to track down news stories, write and edit copy, and report
their stories on the air.

Here are some descriptions of a variety of interesting television
news jobs:

News Director

This department head manages a staff of news anchors, reporters,
editors, producers, camera operators, technicians, and assistants.
The position requires a communications degree, at least five years'
experience in reporting and evaluating news, plus leadership skills,
experience, and expertise in administrative, financial, and personnel management.

Assistant News Director/Assignment Editor

This person is second in command in the news department. He or
she supervises the newsroom staff, makes assignments, solves problems as they arise, and assists the news director in long-range
planning. Job requirements are a journalism or broadcasting degree,
at least three years of TV news experience, and management
potential.

News Producer/Director

The producer/director is responsible for the planning, preparation,
and production of television newscasts. This is a graphics-intensive,
complex process that requires a clear, cool head, imaginative showmanship, and sound news judgment.

News Production Assistant

Duties of this job vary according to the needs of the senior producer but may include checking out news tips, writing and rewriting news, editing and timing news tapes, and assembling newscast segments. A college degree and previous broadcast news experience is required.

News Reporter

A TV news reporter covers local news—everything from fires and murders to meetings with the mayor and civic club luncheons. The job requires skills in interviewing and in interpreting information.

The ability to write and speak well, as well as proficiency in the use of cameras, recorders, and electronic transmission devices, are also essential. To qualify you should have a degree in electronic communications.

News Anchor

This person is the personality around whom a major TV newscast is built. The news anchor reads news items and introduces live and taped inserts by other reporters and correspondents. This coveted position pays well but demands proven skills as a news communicator.

Duties may include investigative reporting; interviewing; writing news; editing copy and video; hosting discussions, debates, and documentaries; making speeches and personal appearances; and participating in TV station promotion and public service campaigns.

Job requirements include a college degree, several years of TV news experience, and the ability to look and sound pleasant and authoritative. Average annual compensation is $73,000, but pay in larger markets exceeds $100,000. Some senior anchors make $250,000 to $1 milion or more.

News Photographer/Cameraperson

A news photographer covers news live with an electronic news gathering (ENG) camera or uses a camcorder to tape reports. In addition to photographic responsibilities, duties may include writing and reporting news stories and editing tapes. Qualifications required are a high school diploma plus previous photographic or television news experience.

Sports Director/Sports Anchor

This person is responsible for sports news and play-by-play coverage presented by a television station. He or she may be required to carry a camera and shoot interviews or sports events live or on tape.

Job requirements are a college degree, knowledge of sports, and the ability to communicate with accuracy and authority.

Meteorologist

The meteorologist collects, analyzes, and reports weather information. Added importance is attached to the position when the forecaster is a certified meteorologist.

News Writer

This job exists mainly at networks and stations that present news 24 hours a day. Responsibilities are primarily to write, edit, and rewrite news stories based on information supplied by reporters, correspondents, and wire services. The resulting copy is used on newscasts, documentaries, and news specials. Job requirements are a journalism/broadcast degree and superior news writing skills.

News Graphics Artist

This person creates the lettering, designs, identifications, graphs, cartoons, and other visual effects that illustrate a news presentation. The job requires news judgment, computer graphics skills, and creative artistry.

News Archivist/Librarian

The person in this job is responsible for indexing and filing news tapes and maintaining an inventory of every sound bite, prominent person, and important news event in the station's archive so it can be quickly recalled when needed.

A high school diploma is required, and technical training is helpful. The job also demands experience in the operation of recording and editing machines and other audiovisual equipment.

News Technician/Video Coordinator

This job exists in busy news operations that require their own technicians. Major areas of responsibility may involve equipment maintenance as well as assignments both in the studio and on location.

The job requires technical training or a degree, plus several years' experience in radio or TV engineering. In addition to news training and experience, this reporter can benefit from being a versatile performer and storyteller.

News Assistant

This entry-level position enables a beginner to learn what television news is all about. Duties may include answering phones, filing news scripts, and doing general secretarial chores. Promotion to a higher paying job depends on demonstrated dependability and proficiency.

A high school diploma is acceptable, but college training is preferred. News assistants should have typing and word-processing skills. Many TV news departments hire student interns for this job. Salaries for beginners are modest, averaging about $200 to $250 a week. Experienced assistants make $15,000 to $20,000 a year.

News Specialist

Television has cultivated a number of news and information jobs, each of which calls for extensive knowledge of a particular subject. Newscasts commonly feature experts on consumer affairs, financial management, personal health, urban problems, environmental science, politics, and military affairs. Some specialists are full-time staff employees, but many work as freelancers on a contract basis. TV news specialists generally have achieved professional success and recognition as authorities in their fields. They also have good communications skills.

Weekend News Jobs

As an economical measure, many TV news operations hire people to work weekends only as news anchors, reporters, videographers, and producers. Since this is part-time employment, it is possible to fill such a position and hold another job elsewhere. Educational and professional qualifications are the same as for full-time employees. The pay is about $100 per day.

Tables 6.1, 6.2, and 6.3 show the staff sizes and salaries for various news staff positions in commercial news and designated market areas (DMA). There are 210 designated market areas throughout the United States.

Table 6.1 TV Staff Size

	Average Total	*Median Total*	*Maximum Total*
All TV News	35.2	31	130
Big Four Affiliates	36.8	32	130
Other Commercial	31.5	31	85
DMA 1–25	62.3	52	130
DMA 26–50	51.8	50	124
DMA 51–100	38.9	38.5	77
DMA 101–150	25.8	26	49
DMA 151+	19.5	18	54

Source: RTNDA/Ball State University 2002 Staffing/Amount of News Research

Table 6.2 Median Television News Salaries, 1996 to 2001

	2001	*1996*	*% Change*
Assistant News Director	$57,000	$44,500	+28.1
News Director	64,000	50,500	+26.7
Weathercaster	43,800	35,000	+25.1
News Anchor	50,000	40,000	+25.0
Sports Reporter	25,000	20,000	+25.0
Photographer	25,000	20,000	+25.0
News Writer	27,500	23,000	+19.6
News Reporter	26,000	22,000	+18.2
Executive Producer	47,000	40,000	+17.5
Assignment Editor	30,000	26,000	+15.4
Internet Specialist	30,000	26,000	+15.4
Sports Anchor	35,000	30,500	+14.8
News Producer	27,000	24,000	+12.5
Managing Editor	50,000	44,500	+12.4
News Assistant	21,000	19,000	+10.5
Tape Editor	23,000	22,000	+4.5
Graphics Specialist	25,000	25,000	0

Source: RTNDA/Ball State University Annual 2002 Radio and Television Salary Survey

Table 6.3 Median TV News Salaries by Market Size (Thousands)

	1–25	26–50	51–100	101–150	150+
News Director	$140,000	$98,000	$75,000	$55,000	$46,500
Assistant News Director	102,500	65,000	55,000	43,000	44,000
Managing Editor	78,300	50,000	44,000	37,500	44,500
Executive Producer	78,000	55,000	45,000	35,000	29,000
Assignment Editor	48,000	35,000	32,000	26,500	24,000
News Producer	49,000	32,500	28,000	21,500	20,000
News Anchor	121,500	60,000	39,000	30,000	25,000
Weathercaster	94,500	50,000	38,500	25,500	20,000
Sports Anchor	97,500	45,000	30,000	25,000	21,000
News Reporter	52,200	30,000	23,000	20,000	19,500
News Writer	38,000	23,000	19,000	*	*
News Assistant	30,000	20,000	14,000	*	*
Sports Reporter	49,000	26,000	20,500	18,500	21,000
Photographer	41,800	25,000	21,000	19,500	19,000
Tape Editor	33,800	21,800	18,000	15,000	*
Graphics Specialist	37,500	30,000	24,000	25,500	*
Internet Specialist	35,000	29,000	32,500	*	*

* Insufficient Data

Source: RTNDA/Ball State University Annual 2002 Radio and Television Salary Survey

Radio News

Nine out of ten stations claim to have news departments. But more often than not, just one full-time employee staffs the department. The remaining news duties are handled by part-timers or announcers who also act as newscasters. Radio stations that are news-active have an average of five employees—a news director, two reporters, and two news announcers.

Salary levels in radio news remain low (see Tables 6.4, 6.5, and 6.6). Still, radio news continues to attract young men and women because it goes where the action is, relaying to the public live reports of what is happening locally and around the world. There are some seven hundred all-news operations in the United States, and several thousand others use radio cars, helicopters, and airplanes to cover local news, traffic, and special events. Since this type of journalism combines speed, simplicity, and availability to mobile listeners, as well as those in homes and workplaces, radio news will continue to be an important broadcast service and a good training ground for news-minded young people.

Table 6.4 Radio News Salaries

	Average	*Median*	*Minimum*	*Maximum*
News Director	$31,000	$30,500	$10,000	$72,000
News Anchor	30,500	27,500	10,000	150,000
News Reporter	22,600	22,000	12,000	42,000
News Producer	29,400	27,500	21,000	42,000
Sports Anchor	28,000	29,500	14,000	50,000

Source: RTNDA/Ball State University Annual 2002 Radio and Television Salary Survey

Table 6.5 Median Radio News Salaries, 1996 to 2000

	2001	*1996*	*% Change*
News Director	$30,500	$23,000	+32.6
News Anchor	27,500	21,000	+31.0
News Producer	27,500	22,000	+25.0
Sports Anchor	29,500	24,000	+22.9
News Reporter	22,000	20,000	+10.0

Source: RTNDA/Ball State University Annual 2002 Radio and Television Salary Survey

Table 6.6 Median Radio News Salaries by Market Size

	Major	*Large*	*Medium*	*Small*
News Director	$46,000	$33,000	$28,500	$23,000
News Anchor	38,500	29,000	24,000	22,000
News Reporter	34,900	22,000	21,000	18,500
News Producer	37,000	*	26,500	23,000
Sports Anchor	35,000	29,500	25,000	*

* Insufficient Data

Source: RTNDA/Ball State University Annual 2002 Radio and Television Salary Survey

News Director

This job requires a solid journalism or broadcasting education, management capabilities, and several years of news writing and reporting experience. Where a radio news staff is small, the news director may handle most responsibilities, including reporting, editing, newscasting, and monitoring breaking news. Table 6.7 lists other responsibilities of radio news directors.

News Reporter

This job provides the kind of experience needed to become a news director or news anchor. The active, daily routine involves checking out news tips, interviewing news sources, writing and editing news copy, and reporting live or on tape. Reporters at most radio stations also deliver newscasts.

News Anchor

The job requires preparing and delivering newscasts from wire copy, local stories, and live and taped reports. Because of limited personnel, anchors commonly do reporting, writing, editing, and other on-air work in addition to their newscasts.

Table 6.7 What Else Do News Directors Do?

Announcing	28.8%
Public Affairs	16.2%
Programming	13.5%
Sports	11.7%
Operations	4.5%
Sales	3.6%
Production	2.8%
Other	18.9%

Source: RTNDA/Ball State University Annual Survey: 2002 Staffing/Amount of New Research

Sports Director

The sports director is responsible for covering sports news and athletic events, including live play-by-play, interviews, and taped reports.

News Editor/Writer

This job exists in all news stations, services, and networks. Most radio stations expect reporters and anchors to do their own writing and editing. Prerequisites are a college degree in journalism or broadcasting and proven ability to write and edit news.

Traffic Reporter

Some stations employ one or more reporters to monitor traffic conditions and make periodic reports, particularly during morning and afternoon rush hours. Surveillance is maintained from a helicopter, airplane, or automobile. Prerequisites are a college education and news experience.

Cable News

Whereas viewers once watched one or two television newscasts a day at specified times, millions now turn to all-news channels and catch up on what's happening at any moment—day or night. The popularity of 24-hour cable news has spawned scores of specialized news services and created numerous jobs, especially for authorities on various subjects such as medicine, music, military affairs, law, economics, government, environmental science, entertainment, sports, and weather.

Television stations, newspapers, and other media have also created a number of news jobs that use cable channels to expand their coverage. Your prospects for cable news employment will be enhanced if you can suggest interesting new ways to report pertinent information. Because news departments have made a transition from analog to digital systems, the need to produce high-quality presentations will stimulate even more electronic news employment.

A word of caution: Many cable news sources stress immediacy and sensationalism. This type of fragmented, disjointed journalism is often without context and is sometimes of questionable news value. You should avoid any tempting offers to engage in this kind of reporting and look for a position with a cable operation that deals in reputable journalism.

Business News Jobs

The stock market attracts millions of investors, and the public is generally interested in receiving periodic reports from Wall Street and foreign markets, as well as other pertinent financial information. Business news has become a regular daily feature on TV, radio, cable, and the Internet. Several cable networks report financial news around the clock, including continuous updates on the value of various stocks, bonds, and currencies.

Numerous local and network programs feature discussion and analysis of what's happening in commerce, industry, and the world's money markets. Since business news has become such a popular topic, demand has increased for financial news reporters. You should have a degree in commerce and news reporting experience to qualify for this position. Pay ranges from $25,000 to $75,000 and up.

Career Advice from News Experts

Here is a sample of what various experts have to say about the field of news reporting and broadcasting:

Q. What is the reporter's role in society?

A. Sam Donaldson, *20/20* correspondent and co-anchor of *This Week with Sam Donaldson and Cokie Roberts* on ABC: "I always thought the reporter's role was to find out what was happening and report that to an audience. That role continues. But how we find out what is happening and how we report it is changing rapidly. Technology is one thing. News can now be broadcast instantly worldwide. And getting a story requires greater sophistication and understanding and research. But the basic function of a reporter—to find out what is going on in the laboratory, in the workplace, in the political forum—has not changed. Good journalism survives if journalists have the wit to adapt to changing times."

Q. Has the reporter's role changed since you became a network news anchor in 1962?

A. Walter Cronkite, former CBS News anchorman: "It's changed in a couple of ways. One, because our news personalities are more personally known now, so that has changed the perception of the news considerably. It's become far more personal than it was before. Also in some ways the responsibility of the press is greater, particularly in our presidential politics, but to a degree in other politics as well. Also, consumer journalism has become a major part of journalistic responsibility, which it never was before. I mean talking about products and their efficiency or their failure. And that's cast a new light on journalistic responsibility, which I think is fine."

Q. What lessons have you learned about the art of interviewing?

A. Mike Wallace, co-editor of *60 Minutes* on CBS: "The importance of research and the importance of listening. By the time you've written several dozen questions, you've done enough research so that you have a fair understanding of almost anything that comes up."

Q. *Is new technology affecting the broadcasting of news?*

A. Hugh Downs, former co-host of *20/20* on ABC: "It has particularly affected the speed with which we can get something on the air; some of the ways we present material to make sure the audience is with us. I think that is for the better, but there is a downside. I think the public suffers from information overload. But on balance I would say it's an asset."

Q. *How do you think news will be reported in the next ten years?*

A. Tim Russert, MSNBC anchor and *Meet the Press* moderator: "It will continue to be rapid and simultaneous in any breaking crisis. It will continue to expand. I believe there will be more and more narrowcasting as people have access to hundreds of cable stations and satellite dishes. And the Internet will continue to thrive."

Q. *Do you recommend continuing education for a newsperson?*

A. Bettina Luscher, CNN Berlin bureau chief: "I am still profiting from the two years I spent studying politics at the University of Wisconsin in Madison; an opportunity granted to me by a scholarship from the Fulbright Foundation. The scholarship gave me more insight into America and taught me always to look at something from various points of view, to get the news across so that it is understandable for every country in the world."

Q. *What changes in news reporting have you experienced?*

A. Rita Braver, senior correspondent for *CBS News Sunday Morning*: "Advances in technology from film to videotape, and from hard-line to satellite, make it quicker and easier to get news on the air than any of us ever dreamed would be possible. And that means the burden is increasing to be careful, to try to put a story into context, to try to convey to the public that we don't know it all, but are just trying to give the best picture of what is going on at the time."

Internet Employment

When the Internet bubble burst in the late 1990s and sparked an economic downturn that lasted several years, many television and radio stations backed away from their Web development plans. Although Internet jobs were available, their numbers were far fewer than they were earlier in the 1990s. Web employees were laid off to keep as many staff reporters and photographers as possible working in the field.

As the economic outlook improves, Internet news jobs have picked up as well. According to the Radio-Television News Directors Association and Foundation (RTNDA), Web staff numbers were higher than ever at television and radio stations at the end of 2002. Because most large stations had already developed websites and employed Internet personnel, the bulk of the growth came from small stations that were starting from scratch.

The overall number of television stations that had a website increased from 91.3 percent at the end of 2001 to 94 percent the following year. In the radio industry, the year over year increase was 67.7 percent in 2001 to 82.7 percent in 2002.

The number of television websites that included news decreased from 93.4 percent to 88.4 percent between 2001 and 2002. Radio increased from 31.7 percent at the end of 2001 to 41.7 percent the following year. By the start of 2003, television stations in all markets had an average of 2.69 people dedicated to the Web on staff, while radio had an average of 2.08 Web employees. Other staff members contributed to Web development and content.

The following are brief descriptions of various Web-related news jobs.

Online News Director

This website position is similar to that of a TV/radio news director or the managing editor at a newspaper. In addition to supervising reporters, photographers, and other news personnel, the news director may also write, edit, and interview subjects. Salaries for online news directors range from $25,000 at small websites to $100,000 or more at major Internet news centers.

Online Reporter

A website reporter gathers and writes news much like a television or print reporter. However, since most Internet news staffs are small, a Web reporter also may have duties as a proofreader, copywriter, editor, columnist, or graphic artist. In markets of equal size, salaries for reporters average about the same as those paid by television stations.

Webmaster

This person is qualified by training and experience to create websites and is often a certified professional in the design, organization, and operation of both local-area and wide-area computer systems. Salaries vary depending on experience and performance record, ranging from $35,000 to more than $75,000.

Certified Professional

This professional has been trained, examined, and certified to design, install, operate, and troubleshoot computer software systems. Starting salaries range from $35,000 to $40,000. A technical software specialist with five or more years of experience may earn $50,000 to $60,000 or more.

Network Engineer

This position requires training and experience in setting up and overseeing the operation of interactive computer systems and networks. Pay averages $70,000 to $80,000.

7

Electronic Media

IT IS WISE for anyone contemplating a career in any form of broadcasting or narrowcasting to be prepared to operate in a highly competitive and somewhat unpredictable environment. Most electronic communicators create their own job security by being so capable and dependable that their employers consider them indispensable. Don't consider electronic media as the key to fame and fortune. Few jobs in broadcasting and narrowcasting are high-salaried, on-camera positions. Most men and women in the industry are content to work behind the scenes.

As in other professions, the most successful and satisfied employees in electronic media are those who are serious about communicating in a clear, correct, and concise fashion. They exhibit creativity and self-reliance, but do so within the boundaries of management's policies and their own sound judgment.

Weighing Your Media Options

There are many logical reasons to study and prepare for a career in electronic communications, especially if you are interested in creating and sharing knowledge with others. This is what communications is all about. The avenues of electronic expression available to you are multiplying rapidly, providing a variety of video and audio channels for interacting with the public in a personal and intimate manner.

A television station can be a stimulating workplace, a vital news-and-information center, and an influential participant in community affairs. As a TV employee, you will meet interesting people and make contacts that may be helpful to your career.

Perhaps you will choose radio as the place to launch your broadcast career. A progressive radio station is in constant contact with listeners throughout its coverage area, and its programming reflects their interests and concerns. Working in this type of operation can make for a job that is richly satisfying.

There are other options, too. Job opportunities at websites and in cable television are growing along with an expanding list of channels, networks, and cable programming services. Numerous other organizations such as TV production studios, educational institutions, advertising and public relations firms, medical facilities, government agencies, public utilities, and private corporations employ a number of people in the creation, development, sales, and distribution of broadcast materials.

On the negative side, not all broadcasting stations or video facilities are pleasant places to work. Some are crowded, cluttered, and poorly maintained. Staff members in some instances work long shifts and odd hours for minimal compensation and have little or no job security.

With deregulation of broadcasting, many owners concentrate on buying and selling stations instead of operating them as a service to the public and a long-term business investment. When a station changes hands, it is not unusual for people to lose their jobs.

On the other hand, many managers go out of their way to be fair and to retain employees by letting them know they are appreciated. A number of companies will pay tuition and expenses for selected personnel to take special courses or attend seminars and conferences.

When interviewing for a job, it is wise to inquire about employee benefits, particularly medical care, stock options, retirement provisions, and self-improvement classes. Keep in mind, though, that it is more important to emphasize the contributions you are prepared to make than to dwell on what an employer has to offer you. Your chances of getting a good job and keeping it will depend primarily on your willingness to give the best that you have to offer, cheerfully and consistently.

Electronic Media in Canada

More than ten thousand men and women in Canada hold various commercial and noncommercial broadcasting jobs. They work at some 750 AM and FM radio stations, which offer a variety of formats; nearly three hundred television outlets; and numerous cable systems. Thousands of others are employed in such related businesses as websites, film and recording studios, syndication services, postproduction facilities, advertising and public relations agencies, public and private video systems, and satellite and wireless networks.

The Canadian Broadcasting Corporation (CBC), established by the government and publicly owned, operates nationwide English and French TV and AM-FM stereo networks. The Canada Radio-Television and Telecommunications Commission (CRTC) requires that 60 percent of the CBC's schedule from 6:00 A.M. to midnight be Canadian.

Private television stations, ethnic stations, and networks such as CTV, Global, and TVA provide similar programming percentages during the year. The CRTC will certify a program as Canadian if the producer is Canadian, key creative personnel are Canadian, and 75 percent of service and postproduction costs are paid to Canadians.

Commercial radio networks in Canada also operate under guidelines that are designed to promote Canadian content and support the country's artists and recording industry. At least 35 percent of popular music selections broadcast from Canada-based AM and FM commercial radio stations each week must be Canadian selections. This percentage of selections must be played between 6:00 A.M. and 6:00 P.M. Monday through Friday to ensure that a high number of listeners are exposed to Canadian artists.

To determine whether radio content qualifies as Canadian, the CRTC devised a four-part system called MAPL, which stands for music, artist, production, and lyrics, to identify Canadian content. If two or more of the following criteria are met, the content is considered Canadian:

1. **Music.** The music is composed entirely by a Canadian.
2. **Artist.** The music is, or the lyrics are, performed principally by a Canadian.
3. **Production.** The musical selection consists of a live performance that is recorded wholly in Canada or performed wholly and broadcast live in Canada.
4. **Lyrics.** The lyrics are written entirely by a Canadian.

There are no restrictions on U.S. citizens seeking employment in a Canadian communications facility. Methods of operation, working conditions, equipment, and benefits are similar to those in the United States, but salaries do not average quite as high. Some media jobs in Canada require that you speak both English and French, and it will be helpful to know something about Canadian history, geography, and politics.

Working in Canada can be a satisfying experience. Unlike the United States, a number of TV and radio stations in Canada still feature locally produced dramas, comedy, musical concerts, documentaries, discussions, and variety shows.

For more information about jobs, check with employment agencies in principal Canadian cities, surf the Web for job listings, or contact any of these organizations:

Canadian Association of Broadcasters
306–350 Sparks Street
Ottawa, Ontario K1R 7S8
Canada
cab-acr.ca
E-mail: cab@cab-acr.ca

Canadian Broadcasting Corporation
250 Lanark Avenue
P.O. Box 3220, Station "C"
Ottawa, Ontario K1Y 1E4
Canada
cbc.ca
E-mail: commho@cbc.ca

Canadian Cable Television Association
360 Albert Street, Suite 1010
Ottawa, Ontario K1R 7X7
Canada
ccta.ca
E-mail: ccta@ccta.ca

Canadian Film and Television Production Association (CFTPA)
    Ottawa
151 Slater Street, Suite 605
Ottawa, Ontario K13 5H3
Canada
cftpa.ca
E-mail: ottawa@cftpa.ca

Canadian Film and Television Production Association (CFTPA)
    Toronto
160 John Street, 5th Floor
Toronto, Ontario M5V 2E5
Canada
cftpa.ca
E-mail: toronto@cftpa.ca

Canadian Film and Television Production Association (CFTPA)
    Vancouver
1140 Homer Street, Suite 301
Vancouver, British Columbia V6B 2X6
Canada
cftpa.ca
E-mail: vancouver@cftpa.ca

Ask the Professor

If the prospect of someday being an electronic media professional excites your imagination and curiosity, you should make an effort to find out as much as possible about broadcasting and narrowcasting. Make appointments with communications specialists who have many years of experience. They may be able to help you choose a profession that is suited to your talent and interests by answering questions and concerns that are on your mind.

Dr. Barry L. Sherman, professor of broadcasting and director of the Peabody Awards at the University of Georgia, has counseled hundreds of students about electronic communications careers. Here are his responses to some of the questions he is most often asked:

Q. How can I best prepare for a career in television, cable, radio, or some other form of electronic communications?

A. The best preparation begins with a college degree. Plan to major in mass communications, journalism, speech communications, or broadcasting at a four-year institution whose program ranks high with the Association for Education in Journalism, the Broadcast Education Association, and other academic and professional authorities.

Q. What do colleges offer that's so valuable?

A. In addition to academic instruction, they provide access to a wealth of extracurricular activities. Most modern universities have campus radio and television facilities, campus newspapers and other publications, speech and debate societies, drama and film groups, and so on. You can learn a lot by taking full advantage of these opportunities.

Q. *How important are internships?*

A. Most seniors in electronic media complete at least one internship at a broadcast/cable outlet before graduation. These days, simply having a degree isn't enough. Many employers consider an internship a better learning experience than working as a part-time employee.

Q. *Are there certain books or courses that you recommend to students of electronic media?*

A. Rather than list specific books or courses, to be well prepared you should place equal emphasis on so-called "theory" and "production" courses. Students often spend too much time in classes that focus on entry-level skills, while neglecting study of writing, critical thinking, history, and broad liberal arts subjects. In general, you need course work in media history, technology, law and policy, social impact and effects, production, advertising, and marketing. You also might consider a minor or elective course in business, political science, speech communications, drama, and international relations.

Q. *What technical skills must I develop?*

A. All media students should know how to operate basic equipment associated with programming and production at radio and television stations. What's more, you will be expected to keep up with new and emerging technology.

Q. *Do you advise consulting or networking with media professionals?*

A. Yes. Mentoring, networking, and other forms of informal contact are often critical to finding a first job and continuing up the career ladder. As has always been the case, it doesn't hurt to know people in the business who are smart, successful, and willing to share what they know with you.

Valuable Communications Qualities

Emerging technologies continue to change the specifications for various kinds of electronic media jobs. But a basic requirement for all positions is the ability to communicate. Many of the qualities that will enable you to communicate successfully are similar to those that a wise manager should look for when hiring any employee. These include good work habits, sound judgment, enthusiasm, patience, a sense of humor, empathy, a personal commitment to excellence, and a sincere desire to understand and be understood.

How do you develop these qualities? Some must emanate naturally from your own positive attitude and desire to succeed. Others can be learned through study, observation, and experience. Getting a well-rounded education in both communications courses and the liberal arts will give you knowledge, awareness, and confidence. An internship will teach you how to use state-of-the-art communications technology and improve your ability to think, speak, and write clearly.

As you prepare for the future, keep an open mind about the direction in which a communications career may lead you. Many students who major in broadcasting don't go to work for a TV or radio station. They find employment in cable operations, production studios, computer systems, nonbroadcast video and audio, satellite delivery, and scores of other businesses.

Colleges of communications are stressing the importance of being versatile and knowing how to do more than one kind of work. As a result, broadcast majors commonly include among their elective courses classes in computer technology, sales, promotion, advertising, marketing, research, and management.

Knowledge of multiple disciplines will give you an advantage in locating a good job. Continually learning new and better ways to do your job will help you to remain employed. Many employers place more emphasis on how adaptable you are to change than on what you already know.

Accordingly, to enhance your career in communications you should strive to develop the following characteristics:

- Readiness to accept advice, coaching, feedback, and responsibility
- Willingness to collaborate and cooperate as an interdependent team member
- Ability to analyze and solve problems
- Technical ingenuity and efficiency
- Initiative
- Dependability
- Business acumen and financial management expertise
- Leadership potential

By combining the right qualities with a solid practical education, you can multiply your career opportunities and strengthen your qualifications for moving up to positions of greater responsibility and higher authority.

Job Satisfaction

Research indicates that most electronic media employees have strong ties to their jobs and dedication to the duties they are hired to perform. They enjoy participating in a high-tech environment, producing and distributing various types of information, entertainment, products, and services to the public.

Interviews conducted with communications professionals indicate a high degree of loyalty to the firms for which they work and the industry they represent. This is an impressive endorsement since compensation, benefits, and job security in the communications industry are often less than in other fields. Apparently, material considerations are less important than the strong desire to work with like-minded associates in a dynamic and vitally important profession.

Electronic Media Career Test

How likely are you to succeed in this business? One way to help you find out is to answer the following questions. On a piece of paper, create three columns titled "Yes," "No," and "Not Sure." As you read each statement, place a check mark in the appropriate column as it applies to you.

1. I am keenly interested in TV, radio, cable, and other forms of electronic communications.
2. I enjoy reading about electronic media.
3. I have visited radio, TV, and cable operations.
4. I know how to operate a camcorder.
5. I can type and use a word processor.

6. I know how to use a computer.
7. I like music and have some musical knowledge.
8. I listen to the radio and watch TV nearly every day.
9. I like to learn about new technologies.
10. I often check to see what's new on cable channels.
11. I have sought career advice from one or more communications professionals.
12. I enjoy meeting and talking with people.
13. I frequently see and hear things on TV that I would like to change or improve.
14. Being a TV or radio performer sounds exciting, but I prefer some other kind of electronic media job.
15. I am a creative person.
16. I consider myself an attentive listener.
17. When assigned a task, I make sure I understand how to do it before I start.
18. I am interested in learning new and better ways of doing things.
19. I enjoy telling others about things I've learned.
20. If I have a deadline to meet, I meet it.
21. I am striving to become a competent writer.
22. I am trying to learn how to be a good public speaker.
23. I do quite well in spelling and geography.
24. When criticized, I listen and try to learn.
25. I enjoy reading both fiction and nonfiction.
26. Listening is as important in communication as talking.
27. I am interested in other people's opinions.
28. I keep up with local, national, and foreign news.
29. I have studied a foreign language.
30. Selling and communicating are related functions.

31. I am inclined to ask a lot of questions.
32. Freedom of press doesn't mean freedom from responsibility for what I say.
33. I have many interests.
34. Excuses are embarrassing, so I try to avoid them.
35. I make written notes of things I have to do.
36. I tend to explain things logically and briefly.
37. I usually manage to stay calm under pressure.
38. Meeting and chatting with strangers appeals to me.
39. Working long hours doesn't bother me.
40. I am pretty good at fixing things and making repairs.
41. Every employee of a business has a duty to help make it profitable and successful.
42. In electronic media—as in any business—the main objective should be to satisfy the customer.
43. Making a lot of money is not my greatest ambition.
44. All jobs in an organization are related and interdependent.
45. I work well without needing close supervision.
46. Communication is a sharing and caring process.
47. Praise, when I have earned it, is worth more to me than money.
48. I am a neat, clean, well-mannered person.
49. I can keep a secret.
50. As a student, I have received more A's and B's than C's and D's.

Score 2 points for every "Yes" answer. A score of 75 or more indicates a high degree of aptitude for a career in electronic media.

8

PREPARING FOR A CAREER IN ELECTRONIC MEDIA

As YOU CONSIDER becoming a broadcaster or narrowcaster, it is logical to ask some basic questions: What jobs are available? How do you qualify for them? How much money can you make? Will you be eligible for any special rewards or benefits? Are you likely to be proud and satisfied working as an electronic communicator? Answers to these concerns are generally positive and encouraging.

Employers are looking for qualified applicants to fill job openings at all levels in radio and television. A number of websites (listed in Appendix B) provide detailed information about jobs in the ever-expanding world of electronic communications. Visiting several of these should be a good starting point in your career preparation.

You also should make an effort to observe firsthand the jobs that electronic communicators hold and the work they do. Contact local radio stations, television stations, cable companies, and websites. Ask to talk with managers and members of their staffs about their operations and learn how various jobs relate to one another.

Check the telephone book for names of other concerns that are engaged in some form of electronic communications, such as production studios, public and private video systems, and telemarketers. Visit them and broaden your knowledge of the interrelated communications facilities.

Decide what kind of work interests you most and best fits your talents and temperament. Are you inclined toward management, sales, engineering, research, marketing, writing, production, or performance? Once you have made a tentative choice, you can ask professionals in that field how you should prepare to do their work.

Regardless of the career choice you make, finding a good job will be easier if you are properly educated and have some on-the-job training or experience. Retaining your position and getting promoted will depend in large measure on how well you carry out your daily communications responsibilities.

A career in media holds promise of both tangible and intangible rewards. Some communications moguls such as Ted Turner and Rupert Murdoch have amassed enormous fortunes. But they are the exception, and most media professionals earn a comfortable living. More important than money is the knowledge that they are engaged in an interesting and vitally important profession.

As a professional communicator, you should be able to exchange and share information and opinions in a clear and concise manner. Improve your public speaking by joining a debate team or drama club. Experiment with speaking extemporaneously while facing a full-length mirror. Get acquainted with communications technology so you know the tools of the trade and how they are used.

Above all, never stop learning and thinking creatively. All forms of electronic media are looking for persons with bright minds and fresh ideas.

Smaller Markets

A common complaint among broadcasters in smaller communities is the difficulty they have in attracting qualified personnel. Many newcomers to the profession apparently want to work only in major markets and choose to be unemployed unless they can find the high-salaried position they have in mind.

If the only job available pays a modest salary and is in a small market, you should accept it and work hard to excel at it. It beats not working at all. Besides, working in a small- or medium-sized community offers certain advantages. Very likely you'll be able to gain a wealth of practical experience that you can use to further your career. This is the route that many professionals have followed to become managers or owners of broadcasting facilities.

So don't be reluctant to start at the bottom, and think twice before leaving a job prematurely to accept another that pays a few more dollars. Take time to get acquainted with the organization you work for. Study how it operates. Learn as much as you can about the organization's management philosophy and commercial practices. As you gain experience and demonstrate your worthiness, other offers may come your way. You may decide to make a move if it fits with your career objectives. On the other hand, you may choose to stay where you are or start your own communications business.

What Management Wants

Radio managers want people who are multitalented. Small staffs and lean budgets favor those who can just as easily announce and report news as they can sell advertising, write copy, and operate equipment.

TV stations, cable companies, and video systems also tend to hire people who can handle multiple responsibilities. In small operations it is common to work in several different areas such as news, sales, production, computer graphics, and traffic.

Like all businesses, electronic media companies want their employees to know about economics, money management, research, marketing, sales, computer technology, and the laws of communications.

Whatever your job interests, there is a value in versatility and you should develop more than one skill. Broaden your knowledge and become adept at doing a number of different things. This is particularly important in organizations where a few people take care of all the duties.

Working Conditions

Media companies in the United States generally maintain well-equipped, attractive workplaces. Offices and studios are usually neat and modern. Most operations have lounges and dining areas where food and refreshments are available. Some even provide on-site gymnasiums and libraries.

A number of companies sponsor and support employee clubs, softball and bowling teams, and other activities designed to boost morale and promote a cooperative family spirit. Staff members are often encouraged to participate in community affairs or lead civic, cultural, and charity projects.

A Monday through Friday, forty-hour workweek is standard in the electronic communications industry. Broadcast performers, however, sometimes work six days a week. Split shifts have decreased, but overtime assignments are common.

Most companies grant one week of vacation after six months of employment. This increases to two weeks after a full year, three weeks after five years, and additional weeks of vacation are added in subsequent years. Nearly all broadcast companies allow eight days of paid sick leave annually. A number provide full or partial payment for life insurance, accidental death, dental care, and short- and long-term disability.

Some employers underwrite the cost of awarding a limited number of civic club and professional-association memberships. Many stations also pay tuition for key employees to attend seminars, workshops, and conventions.

Money Matters

Those job-hunting in the competitive world of electronic media should do so for reasons other than getting rich. You can make money more easily in other professions. Even starting salaries for schoolteachers, generally considered to be low, average well above what a typical beginner in broadcasting and narrowcasting receives. However, capable communicators can make a comfortable living.

Something other than money motivates most of the men and women who work as electronic media professionals. Although they are aware that they could earn more in other fields, many newcomers elect to become communicators because it's what they've had a lifelong desire to do.

Education

In this section, you'll find information on the various levels of education, the types of courses you should take, and what kind of career attainment you can expect for each level of educational achievement.

High School

High school is a good place to start preparing for any career. Knowledge and study habits developed in these formative years will prove valuable in the future. Every course you take will add to your storehouse of usable information.

If you plan to work in electronic media, start reading up on the subject. Appropriate books and periodicals can be found at most libraries. Join or organize a communications club. Visit broadcasting stations, cable companies, and related facilities to observe what goes on behind the scenes. Inquire about internships or part-time employment. Nothing beats on-the-job experience.

Trade and Technical Schools

Numerous trade and technical schools offer courses and grant certificates in broadcast engineering, television/radio copywriting, editing, production, sales, communications law, and other related subjects. Courses usually run from six months to one year.

Schools of this type vary in the quality of instruction and equipment. Before enrolling in a course, check to see if the institution is accredited by the National Association of Trade and Technical Schools or licensed by a state board of education. Though not as impressive or valuable as a university degree, trade school training has helped many young men and women launch successful careers. Graduates of these schools frequently get jobs with small companies, gain experience, and eventually move up to better-paying positions.

College and University Training

Although some jobs in electronic media do not require higher education, you will find it much easier to find a job and qualify for a promotion if you have a degree or at least some college education. Advanced schooling is generally required for supervisory and management positions that carry greater responsibilities and offer bigger salaries.

In today's competitive environment, it also is advisable to take refresher courses periodically. Continuing the educational process will make you more knowledgeable and improve your ability to deal with people and problems. Reading in your spare time and attending seminars are other ways to become more proficient.

More than four hundred U.S. colleges and universities confer degrees in broadcasting and communications, and at least 1,200 others offer courses in the field. For a list of 2003–2004 Broadcast Education Association institutional member schools, see Appendix C.

Students pursuing a degree in communications should balance classes in professional practices with an assortment of liberal arts and technical subjects. Some subjects that professional broadcasters encourage students to study include speech, creative writing, history, psychology, economics, law, marketing, financial management, advertising, public relations, research, sales and sales promotion, and computer graphics.

The Accrediting Council on Education in Journalism and Mass Communications recommends that students develop a comprehensive background in government and political science, economics, history, English, American literature and composition, geography, sociology, and at least one foreign language. The organization also stresses the importance of understanding broadcasting as a social instrument and its relationship to government, industry, and the public.

Many colleges and universities offer degrees in computer-based communications. Programs in information technology emphasize development and use of computer-based knowledge and skills to answer expanding communications needs. Graduates with this degree can qualify for high-paying positions in information technology and information systems.

Students who study networking and communications systems learn to analyze the needs of organizations and build networks to meet those needs. Upon graduating they are qualified to be network or system administrators or computer specialists.

Those who major in information technology (IT) management find work as systems analysts, database administrators, end-user support specialists, and information systems managers. Since most businesses utilize computer technology to some extent, positions for IT professionals are available at a number of organizations.

Students who complete courses in multimedia technology acquire competency in designing, developing, and implementing computer-based multimedia programs or websites for clients in such fields as education, marketing, information, and entertainment.

Selecting a College or University

Schools differ considerably in the type and quality of training they offer. For example, some have modern studios and laboratories with state-of-the-art equipment that allows students to work under actual broadcast conditions. Contrast that with institutions that lack such facilities and must create an imaginary newsroom or studio in an ordinary classroom. Better-endowed schools also are more likely to have faculty members with professional experience. This is preferable to being taught by instructors with only textbook knowledge.

Many colleges have radio and television studios on campus. These are excellent places for students to get practical experience by volunteering for work assignments.

Broadcasting Fraternities and Societies

Numerous broadcasting and journalistic organizations that are dedicated to high educational standards and professionalism have members or student chapters on college campuses across the country. Among these are the Society of Professional Journalists (Sigma Delta Chi), American Women in Radio and Television (AWRT), Alpha Epsilon Rho (National Broadcasting Society), Intercollegiate Broadcasting System, Iota Beta Sigma, and National Association of College Broadcasters.

Affiliation with organizations such as these can be an enriching experience that enables students to meet classmates who share common interests and aspirations. After graduating from college, members may elect to affiliate with professional chapters of these organizations.

Internships, Scholarships, and Fellowships

A number of broadcasters, cable companies, and other electronic media offer students on-the-job training and financial assistance. Aid may be provided as internships, co-op employment, scholarships, fellowships, apprentice positions, or grants for research and study projects related to the industry.

Interns customarily work while on vacation from school. Though they receive little or no compensation, students obtain valuable experience and a chance to associate with professionals already working in their chosen field. Any student who wants to apply for an internship can get details from a school counselor or make direct contact with companies that have such programs.

Co-op programs at a number of colleges and universities allow students to alternate between attending classes for one semester and working full-time the next semester. Under this arrangement, participants gain considerable professional experience by the time they receive a degree.

Quite a few TV, radio, and cable companies award scholarships and fellowships. The winners are paid a salary to spend a number of weeks working at broadcast stations and cable systems. Other communications associations, societies, and institutions of higher learning provide scholarship awards and financial assistance programs. For details and contact information regarding scholarships, internships, fellowships, and grants, see Appendix A.

Résumés and Software

A well-crafted résumé communicates in a positive and impressive manner an applicant's academic, professional, and personal qualifications for employment. It is one aspect of your job search over which you have complete control, so it is in your best interest to make your résumé neat, easy to read, and logically arranged.

Computer software is available to simplify résumé writing and ensure a perfect manuscript. With programs such as Microsoft Word you can create a polished résumé and a good cover letter. Have someone you trust proofread what you have written to check for mistakes, omissions, and readability. A poor résumé could cost you a job. A well-prepared résumé may give you the competitive edge you need to be selected for a position.

When applying for an on-air job with a television or radio station, it is a good idea to prepare and submit a video résumé. The video résumé should be concise but filled with pertinent information about your education, training, and broadcasting experience. Insert clips of your performances on actual programs or newscasts. Don't forget to include your address, phone number, and any other information that may highlight your qualifications.

Make sure that your résumé is accurate and carefully worded so that it reads well and sounds natural. Rehearse the script until you feel comfortable with its content and are capable of speaking the lines on camera with clarity and authority.

As you prepare to videotape your résumé, dress neatly and informally just as you would for an in-person interview. When you go before the camera for the actual production, don't slouch, frown, or try to act funny. Remember to look composed, pleasant, and confident.

While producing the video, edit anything that should be corrected, improved, or deleted. You want the finished product to project your words and your image in the best possible light.

Licensing

The Federal Communications Commission (FCC) has liberalized or eliminated licensing requirements for many jobs in radio, television, and other electronic media. A professional technician still must qualify for a general operator's license by passing an FCC test, but on-air personnel no longer need a restricted operator's permit.

Such permits, however, are still available and can be obtained from any FCC field office without submitting to a required test.

How to Get That First Job

"Entry-level positions are not plentiful anywhere in the high-tech communications world, but with proper planning and persistence, jobs can be found," says James W. Wesley Jr., former president of Patterson Broadcasting. Here's his advice to young job hunters:

- Get a good education and, if possible, professional experience working part-time or as an intern.
- Stay informed by reading books, trade papers, and periodicals about the industry. Learn the language of the trade. Keep up with technological progress.
- Develop a specialty. Expertise in computers, science, a foreign language, or some other popular subject may give you an advantage in competing for certain jobs where specialized knowledge is needed.
- Cultivate industry friends. Ask for advice from persons experienced in the kind of work you'd like to do. Join a communications club or association. Attend industry meetings, seminars, and conventions. Monitor the media.
- Be flexible and adaptable. Since job responsibilities are not the same in all organizations, keep an open mind about the position you are after. Be willing to meet any reasonable job requirements.
- Use a variety of approaches in job hunting. Consult with school and library career counselors. Check help-wanted ads in industry publications. Contact employment agencies. Rely on networking with people in the business.

- Prepare a clean, concise, typed résumé, paying close attention to grammar, spelling, and format. If applicable, include samples of your work—even material done as classroom assignments. When submitting a résumé, attach an appropriate typed letter that explains briefly why you want the job.

- Focus on your objective. Decide what state or region you prefer to work in and then investigate job opportunities in that area. Don't apply to a large market for a job you're not qualified to handle. Smaller markets are more likely to hire people with limited or no experience and provide more diversified training.

- Apply with care. Look for organizations that have a good reputation and are known to be in sound financial condition. Select a few of the most promising, send a cover letter and résumé, and ask for an interview. Make sure they know who you are and what you look like. Face-to-face meetings often lead to job offers.

- Prepare for a job interview by anticipating what you may be asked and rehearse proper answers. Dress neatly and appropriately. Be prepared to explain how your abilities can be of value to the organization. Don't go overboard and make extravagant claims or promises. Be enthusiastic, but modest; confident, but respectful.

- Employment beats unemployment. If you can't find a full-time job, look for part-time or temporary employment. Take freelance assignments. This will enable you to earn money and stay active professionally. You're more likely to be offered a job when you are employed than if you are unemployed.

- Don't aim too high or be too demanding. Accept the first reasonable job offer you get. No matter what your ultimate

objective is, you must first get your foot in the door. Be grateful for a modest salary and the chance to gain valuable experience.
- Finally, work hard to earn the respect and confidence of your employer. Be optimistic about the future, and if you are determined to be successful, you very likely will be.

One of the best ways to find a good broadcasting job is through personal contact with people in the business. Cultivate friendships with successful professionals. Seek their advice. If there's a particular organization you want to work for, arrange to visit its headquarters. Spend time learning about its operations and meeting some of its employees.

Commercial firms, government agencies, educational institutions, and professional associations use a variety of media to recruit personnel, including classified ads in newspapers, industry journals, and magazines; websites; and recorded job hotlines. Check these sources regularly.

Millions of career opportunities are listed daily on numerous Internet job sites. Popular sites such as careerbuilder.com and monster.com post job opportunities that are available in many industries and provide résumé advice and career counseling to users. Other sites such as journalismjobs.com, mediabistro.com, and newsjobs.net specialize in media-related jobs and provide industry news. A typical help-wanted ad gives a brief description of the position to be filled, the salary range, and benefits, along with required education, skills, and experience. For a list of job sites on the Web, see Appendix B.

Colleges and universities customarily provide graduates with useful employment and career-advancement guidance. The Web is a convenient way to link up with colleagues and find out about employment opportunities. Another way to learn about job openings is to attend meetings of media professionals. Make networking a part of your daily job-hunting routine.

Many communities operate employment offices, hold job fairs, and provide job-counseling services. Help also is available from state and federal employment agencies. Strategic use of these resources may lead you to a satisfying job and a successful broadcasting career.

9

RADIO

WHEN THE FEDERAL Communications Commission (FCC) deregulated the communications industry with the Telecommunications Act of 1996, aggressive radio groups acquired scores of FM and AM properties. Under the act, companies can own as many as eight in markets with 45 or more commercial radio stations, seven in markets with 30 to 44 stations, six in markets with 15 to 29 stations, and five in markets with fewer than 15 radio stations.

The Telecom Act also eliminated national ownership limitations, removing the 20 AM and 20 FM caps that existed prior to 1996. By 1998 more than one-quarter of all radio stations in the United States were in the hands of a few giant conglomerates.

Multiple station owners can cut expenses and make greater profits by eliminating overlapping staff members, using syndicated services, and relying heavily on automated equipment. Although ownership consolidation has reduced the number of jobs available at individual stations, it has created new opportunities for professionals who are qualified to handle multistation responsibilities in management, programming, sales, marketing, engineering, and promotion.

For example, retail specialists are hired to develop and sell programming features such as outdoor concerts, athletic events, and conventions that are suitable for a group of commonly owned stations.

AM Radio

AM is the oldest system of broadcasting and is often referred to as "standard broadcast." It is designed to convert sounds collected by a microphone into electrical impulses—or audio waves—of varying intensity. These audio waves are amplified and impressed on "carrier waves" that modulate in amplitude to correspond to the strength and frequency of the audio waves they carry or transmit. Thus, the name amplitude modulation, or AM, broadcast.

The FCC has created these AM broadcast channels:

- **Clear Channel.** Stations in this category serve wide areas and are protected from interference within their primary service areas and, in some instances, secondary areas.
- **Regional Channel.** This channel is for class B and class D stations that operate to serve primarily a principal population center and the contiguous rural area.
- **Local Channel.** Local channel stations operate for an unlimited length of time and serve the primary community and the immediately contiguous suburban and rural areas.

Every AM station is assigned an FCC classification. Class A stations operate on a clear channel with power levels between 10,000 watts and 50,000 watts. They have no time restrictions and are designed to provide primary and secondary service to a widespread area. A limited number of clear channel stations have 50-kilowatt transmitters that send out an umbrella pattern of sky-wave and ground-wave signals to local and distant listeners.

Class B stations are designed to provide service only over a primary area. They may operate for an unlimited length of time at power levels between 250 watts and 50 kilowatts. Class B stations in the 1,605 to 1,705-kilohertz band are limited to 10-kilowatt power.

Class C stations operate on a local channel and are designed to render service only over a primary area that may be reduced if interference with other stations occurs. Power in Class C stations ranges from 250 watts to one thousand watts.

Class D stations operate either daytime, limited time, or unlimited time with nighttime power less than 250 watts. Daytime power ranges from 250 watts to 50,000 watts.

FM Radio

Only a handful of scientists knew about frequency modulation (FM) when broadcasting was in its infancy. The general public didn't find out about FM until the 1930s, when Edwin H. Armstrong began trumpeting the superior qualities of FM. It wasn't until 1940 that the FCC allocated 35 channels for commercial FM and 5 for noncommercial, educational FM.

On October 31, 1940, the commission granted construction permits for the first 15 FM stations. By the time World War II halted all such activity, 30 FM outlets were on the air, reaching about 400,000 homes. Growth of FM remained slow for several decades until the public gradually discovered that FM offered high fidelity, clarity, and less static than AM.

The FCC authorized stereo broadcasting in 1961. Since that time, most FM and some AM stations transmit programs in stereo.

Many television stations and cable channels also provide service in stereo to their audiences.

In 1962 the FCC divided the country into three FM zones and created three classes of commercial FM stations: Class A, Class B, and Class C.

Class A stations were assigned to all zones and were permitted a maximum of three kilowatts effective radiated power and maximum antenna height of three hundred feet. Class B stations were assigned to zone I and IA and were allowed a maximum power of 50,000 watts and maximum antenna height of five hundred feet. Class C stations were assigned to zone II and were allowed up to 100 kilowatts of power and maximum antenna height of two thousand feet.

Digital and Satellite Radio

With a few exceptions, the radio industry has clung to its analog roots better than other broadcast mediums have. Whereas analog radio transmits electrical signals that resemble sound waves, digital radio systems process sound into number patterns. Much like music CDs, digital radio reception is clearer, channel programming is more narrowly defined, and it is not impacted by the interference that can disrupt analog radio service.

Satellite radio companies such as XM and Sirius beam signals from 22,000 miles above the Earth to provide digital quality sound. In 2001 and 2002, a small number of automobile manufacturers began outfitting some car models with satellite radio receivers. Unlike analog, signals in cars equipped for satellite radio signal do not fade, and one can drive cross-country without ever losing the signal or ever having to change the station.

Growth of Radio Networks

For many years, four major radio networks—ABC, NBC, CBS, and Mutual—dominated in the United States, each providing hundreds of affiliate stations with a variety of programs. But the coming of television caused radio networks to lose listeners and affiliates. They appeared doomed to extinction.

Interest in radio networks revived, however, when variety programming was abandoned and audio services such as those we hear today were created. As a result, thousands of radio stations are presently affiliated with one or more networks. Many of them are dependent on networks to supply most or all of their daily programming.

Thousands of radio stations aim their programming at specific demographic groups as they strive to reach people of a particular race, age, and socioeconomic level. Radio networks and syndicates, in turn, cooperate by supplying appropriate programming.

It is less expensive to purchase or contract this type of audio service than it is to produce it with local staff talent. Therefore, networks are likely to remain popular with broadcasters, which should mean a sizable number of jobs for persons qualified to develop and market network and syndicated productions (see Table 9.1).

Table 9.1 Radio News Department Staff Size

	Average Staff Size	*Largest Staff Size*
All Radio News	2	21
Major Market	5	21
Large Market	3	18
Medium Market	2	17
Small Market	1	9

Source: RTNDA/Ball State University 2002 Staffing/Amount of News Research

Radio Personalities

Every radio station, whether FM or AM, radiates a distinctive sound and personality. Many factors are involved in creating and maintaining this image to entice listeners and attract advertisers. Foremost in determining a station's personality is its programming.

Thousands of stations depend primarily on the music they play to define them. But competition among stations that use similar music formats can make it difficult to distinguish one from another.

Some stations are known and preferred primarily because of talented performers heard on daily shows. Whether a station relies on talk, music, or a combination of the two, its size and power, management philosophies, marketing methods, or the importance the public places on the service it delivers define its personality.

Job requirements vary among radio stations, depending on the nature of the programming, the sound and image that the facility wants to project, and the demographic segment it is trying to reach. Working as a disc jockey at a youth-oriented station is quite different from being a newscaster or talk show host on an outlet that appeals to adult males who are between the ages of 18 and 34.

There is an obvious need for poorly defined radio stations to work harder at building a positive sound personality. Providing this kind of leadership can open the door to a rewarding radio career.

The Hometown Station

Despite the prevalence of automated radio stations that feature only music, talk, or news, a sizable number of stations continue to deliver live, comprehensive programming that melds various information and entertainment elements into their daily schedule.

Such stations usually subscribe to a radio news service and may affiliate with a national or regional network to fill programming needs. But by and large, a "hometown station" concentrates on being a dependable voice of the community. It is an excellent training ground for beginners in broadcasting.

The radio industry utilizes the wealth of digital technology that is available to gather and air materials for broadcast. Radio professionals use digital equipment to record audio, laptop computers to mix and edit captured sound, and MP3 sound files to produce and present radio programs (see Tables 9.2 and 9.3).

Table 9.2 Percent of News Material Gathered, Edited, and Aired Digitally (Average)

	Gathered	*Mixed and Edited*	*Aired*
All Radio	42.9%	54.4%	55.5%
Major Market	50.1	63.0	55.0
Large Market	42.1	49.5	52.9
Small Market	33.8	45.7	45.9

Source: RTNDA/Ball State University Survey: 2002 Staffing/Amount of News Research

Table 9.3 Percent of Radio News Departments That Gather, Edit, and Air News Digitally

	Gather Some or All	*Edit Some or All*	*Air Some or All*
All Radio	75.9%	71.6%	71.1%
Major Market	85.7	80.0	75.0
Large Market	82.6	73.9	62.5
Medium Market	78.4	74.5	76.5
Small Market	65.9	64.3	66.7

Source: RTNDA/Ball State University Survey: 2002 Staffing/Amount of News Research

Group and Niche Programming

Specialized formats predominate commercial radio station programming in the United States. Most stations transmit and promote a single type of music, designed to appeal to a certain demographic or psychographic segment of the local population. A number of facilities play no music at all, offering instead all talk, news, or sports.

Although the increase in multiple-station ownership resulted in the elimination of jobs and departments, consolidation of ownership isn't entirely bad. More high-salaried positions have opened up for specialists in intermarket programming, syndication, group sales, mini-networks, and promotion.

Relatively few stations continue to provide diversified entertainment, advice, and information. The vast majority now fill a specific programming niche so expertly that they are able to outperform all competitors in this one narrowly focused area. Revenues nationwide indicate positive results from their efforts. The industry is healthy and new stations are steadily being licensed to go on the air.

Automation and Syndication

Thousands of radio stations are now semi-automated or completely automated. Computerized systems regulate the flow of program elements. Networks, program producers, and format providers supply music, talk, news, and features for these mechanized operations.

Syndicated program distribution by satellite, wireless, or other means is a thriving business. Scores of firms are engaged in program production, marketing, merchandising, and bartering. Barter inventory consists of programming or services that syndicators trade to broadcasters in exchange for commercial airtime. The syndicator then sells the bartered airtime to advertisers.

Numerous jobs are available in the syndication industry, especially for those experienced in sales and marketing. There are opportunities as well in developing programs for syndication.

10

Radio Employment

STUDIES INDICATE THAT Americans still depend heavily on radio at home, at work, and in their automobiles. As a result, the radio industry remains strong. One station is often preferred over others because it plays a particular style of music, has a disc jockey who is more likable than others, or offers reliable news, weather, and traffic.

The personal nature of radio broadcasting makes any job in this field challenging. People who work in radio are not isolated observers or detached reporters of the current scene; they are participants with a large following of listeners in a unique communication process. This develops out of the way that radio reaches the mind and stirs the imagination through the sense of sound, making for an intimate, one-to-one relationship.

It's possible that radio's greatest service is the companionship that this localized, mobile, around-the-clock community service provides in the form of news, music, talk, and a host of other formats. It is known that radio stations take on a personality of their own and frequently enjoy the friendship and loyalty of a vast audience.

The most respected station is one at which staff members are deeply involved in the life of the community and reflect this involvement in a variety of attractive and reliable broadcast services.

Many progressive minds in radio have worked to create a dynamic industry that changes constantly to match the needs and desires of the public. There is a profound difference between today's radio programs compared with the radio heard decades ago. Programs today are more explicit and informal than they once were.

In many ways, radio is the most versatile, adaptable, and efficient of all media. Its ability to reach and cater to a multitude of people with instantaneous and ever-changing local service is unique. Anyone who makes radio broadcasting a career choice should understand these characteristics and be prepared to work comfortably and energetically in a profession that emphasizes speed, flexibility, spontaneity, and close contact with the audience.

There has always been a need in radio for people who are talented, sensitive, dependable, and of good character. But the progress of broadcasting calls for more than this. Radio needs imaginative and competitive communicators who believe in the medium and its mission. Radio needs young men and women who want to build a career in radio rather than use it as a stepping-stone to a career in television or another field.

Although job titles and duties vary somewhat, the basic functions of radio operations are quite similar, regardless of station or staff sizes. Beginners can learn broadcasting fundamentals at a small station and later transfer these skills to a bigger station in a larger market, where compensation and working conditions can be more attractive. Such a move is more likely to succeed if the employee has concentrated on gaining valuable experience and practical on-the-job training about the many facets of broadcasting.

Programming and Production

The following are various positions within programming and production:

Program Director

Wherever a radio station originates its own programming, the person responsible for giving the station a popular and distinctive sound is the program director. Working with announcers and other staff members, the program director develops programming targeted toward a particular demographic audience that both the station and its advertisers want to reach.

At many stations, the program director also serves as an announcer, salesperson, satellite-and-computer coordinator, or assistant station manager. At some locations the job entails handling community affairs, automated operations, and personnel matters. The program director of a large station is usually expected to have knowledge of sales, marketing, research, strategic planning, promotions, and budgeting.

Prerequisites include a college degree, preferably in communications; several years of broadcast experience; technical, creative, and leadership skills; and management potential. Salaries range from $40,000 to $300,000, depending on market size. The national average is about $70,000.

Assistant Program Director

A senior staff member often holds this position and helps the program director assign duties within the program department. To qualify, you should have college training and professional experience in programming, sales, and marketing. Salaries range from $25,000 to $35,000.

Music Director

This person selects the songs and artists that a radio station plays. Instead of making arbitrary choices, however, the music director is likely to rely heavily on demographic research, record sales figures, and music popularity charts to decide what music to pick.

Many stations no longer have a staff music director. They contract with companies that supply around-the-clock musical programming on tape or by satellite delivery. To qualify as a music director, you need to know how to select songs that fit a station's format and how to play them by computerized sequencing. Broadcast experience is helpful. The national average salary for a music director is $30,000, but some make $50,000 to $100,000.

Radio Operations Director/Production Manager

The job titles may vary, but the position entails coordinating the creative output of the program, sales, news, and technical departments to make sure the station's programs and commercials are properly produced. Duties may include assigning announcers and producers, troubleshooting production problems, and supervising the operation and maintenance of studios, production equipment, and vehicles.

A liberal arts education, broadcast production experience, and demonstrated management potential are prerequisites for this job. Salaries range from $15,000 to $20,000 in small markets to $50,000 to $75,000 in major ones. The national average salary is about $40,000.

Radio Producer/Director

This job is found most often in radio stations that require a coordination director for morning and afternoon drive-time programs, two-way talk shows, or other programs that require a producer to book guests, screen phone calls, and integrate news, weather, traffic reports, and features into a fast-moving format.

When not on the air, producers write and produce commercials and promotional announcements. On shows that use such material, they often write skits, scan publications for program ideas, suggest publicity stunts and contests, and localize news stories. Material and ideas used in other areas are often adapted for use in their own market. At small stations with simple formats, announcers and disc jockeys serve as their own producers.

A producer/director at larger stations is usually a senior staff member with considerable experience in announcing, writing, news, and commercial production. Salaries can run from $25,000 to $110,000. The national average is $29,000.

Programming/Production Assistant

This position assists the program and production departments. Duties may include serving as director of community affairs and responding to inquiries, requests for assistance, and cooperation on community events and projects. This job also may entail scheduling public service programs and announcements and maintaining records of services rendered to civic groups, schools, religious organizations, charities, and minorities.

You should have a communications degree and be interested in public affairs and community service. A salary of $20,000 to $35,000 is common. The national average is about $30,000.

Disc Jockeys and Drive-Time Talent

Millions of listeners dial in to specific radio stations every day because they prefer to hear certain personalities. Some are hosts of music shows. Others preside over news and talk programs, interviewing guests and chatting about a range of light and serious subjects. Morning drive time is the most valuable period of the broadcast day, and announcers who work these hours normally make the most money. Afternoon drive is the next most important time, followed by nighttime and late-night segments.

Disc jockeys who feature a specific type of music should be friendly and possess a keen sense of humor, a pleasant voice, a good education, and a warm, engaging manner. Talk-show talent must be aware of current affairs and adept at discussing any issues or hot topics that the audience wants to sound off about.

Salaries for on-air talent range from a small-town low of $17,000 to $1 million or more in major markets.

General Announcers

Relatively few people are now employed exclusively as radio announcers. Instead, an employee who can read intelligently and speak clearly may be assigned multiple duties that include announcing, writing and producing commercials, reporting, interviewing, newscasting, and sales. Salaries range from $15,000 to $50,000.

Pay for announcers on morning-drive radio programs varies considerably, depending upon the size of the market, how the stations are formatted, and the popularity of the talent. Few radio performers ever qualify as superstars on a national level. Many local personalities, however, are popular and well paid.

Sales

The American system of commercial radio broadcasting is based on a simple premise: attract listeners with entertainment and information, then sell that audience of listeners to advertisers. This sales effort has become a sophisticated process involving the unified efforts of management, on-air personalities, producers, promotional experts, and salespeople. Together they market the station's tightly formatted sound and service by utilizing demographic data and consumer research, innovative marketing concepts, sales and audience promotion, strong merchandising, and extensive use of other media for advertising and publicity.

Radio revenues come from five principal advertising sources: local, regional, national, co-op, and network. A station's sales staff or its sales representatives sell local, regional, national, and co-op advertising. Network compensation comes from broadcasting commercials or programs a network sells. Positions available in radio sales include the following:

General Sales Manager

This person is the leader of the radio station's sales and marketing team. He or she must be able to recruit, train, and motivate a capable and competitive sales force; identify revenue opportunities; and maximize income. Prerequisites include a business or communications degree and a proven track record of success in sales and management.

Compensation may be by salary, commission, bonus, or any combination thereof. Radio sales managers earn anywhere from $60,000 to $250,000 a year.

Local Sales Manager

The local sales manager is responsible for local advertising revenue. He or she supervises marketing efforts of the local sales staff and may handle some accounts personally. Someone who was promoted from the sales staff usually fills this job. Average earnings nationwide are $95,000 per year. The highest paid can make more than $125,000.

National Sales Manager

The national sales manager is responsible for national advertising revenue. He or she works with the station's national sales representatives to solicit and obtain orders from several large market advertisers. Average compensation for this job is $98,000.

Account Executive/Salesperson

The account executive/salesperson makes sales-and-marketing presentations to businesses and advertising agencies. Duties in small stations may include writing, announcing, and producing commercials once the concept has been sold. A college education is desirable, especially courses in marketing and psychology.

Earnings may come from commissions only or a combination of salary and commission. Account executives earn, on average, $50,000 a year. But incomes of $100,000 or more are not uncommon.

Sales Support

This person provides assistance to the sales managers and account executives, which can include secretarial duties, word processing, and record keeping. Average salary for this job is $24,000.

Radio Continuity Director/Copywriter

This person conceives and writes commercial announcements and other copy, often rapidly and under pressure. Ability to direct and record commercials is another requirement in many stations. Prerequisites are a college degree with emphasis on English, advertising, and broadcasting courses. Average salary is less than $20,000, but experienced professionals usually make $35,000 to $45,000.

Radio Merchandising Manager

The merchandising manager helps advertisers sell their products and services with point-of-purchase displays, sales incentives, on-air contests, sales promotional mailings, and other forms of support and encouragement. Prerequisites for the job are a degree in business or communications, plus training or experience in sales, advertising, and promotion. Salary range is $25,000 to $50,000.

Co-Op Coordinator

This job requires finding out where co-op advertising funds, which are allocated by major suppliers, are available. The coordinator persuades eligible local firms to spend their money on radio.

Sports Sales Specialist

This specialist sells sports sponsorships and commercials for sports events and programs.

Marketing, Promotion, and Publicity

Radio stations use a variety of marketing and promotional techniques to project a distinctive image and attract listeners and advertisers. These efforts involve the use of multimedia and fall into a number of categories—audience promotion, sales promotion, merchandising, publicity, and public relations.

Marketing Director/Promotion Director

This position supervises the station's marketing efforts, working closely with sales, programming, research, promotion, and publicity departments. The director also creates comprehensive sales and audience-building campaigns. Minimum job requirements are a bachelor's degree with courses in broadcasting, advertising, and promotion; strong creative, strategic, and competitive talents; and experience in broadcast promotion.

Marketing/Promotion Assistant

Duties may include working on press releases, radio-TV promotional announcements, advertising campaigns, contests, publicity stunts, special events, merchandising tie-ins, and research projects.

Research

Research has become increasingly important to broadcasters who want to be continually updated on the popularity of music, air personalities, programs, and the relative strength of their competition. Some stations have staff research directors and use research findings for sales and marketing campaigns, but most stations contract with research firms to obtain needed information. Thousands of stations subscribe to Arbitron, Birch, and other research companies for periodic audience-measurement reports.

The research director obtains and analyzes information needed by broadcasters in making programming, sales, and advertising decisions. An undergraduate degree in business administration with emphasis on computerized demographic, psychographic, and marketing research will make job applicants more attractive to employers. Experience in radio sales or programming is also helpful.

Management and Administration

At every radio station, a staff of administrators and their assistants provide leadership, guidance, and support to employees throughout every department. At the top are the owners and managers. Backing them up are specialists in finance, human resources, office services, and maintenance. Included in the general administrative family are secretaries, receptionists, clerks, typists, bookkeepers, and janitors. Together these people answer the phones, sort mail, write letters, buy supplies, collect debts, and pay bills.

Radio Station Owner

Radio stations in the United States are bought and sold almost every day. Federal deregulation has made it relatively easy for anyone with adequate financing to purchase an AM or FM facility.

It is also possible to build a radio station, provided you can find an available frequency. But the search may be slow, expensive, and open to competition from other applicants. It is advisable to have professional broadcast experience before undertaking the responsibilities of ownership.

The radio spectrum is crowded with stations, many of which are not profitable. Those who are up-to-date on broadcast technology, are clever and sensitive programmers, are expert at sales and promotions, and are astute financial managers operate the most successful radio stations.

Radio General Manager/Station Manager

Professionals in these positions select, advise, and motivate department heads to meet the station's goals. They provide strong leadership, especially in sales, and serve as sales managers in many small operations. Other duties include representing the station in dealings with governmental agencies and participating in broadcasting and local civic affairs.

A college degree in communications, plus well-rounded experience in strategic marketing, programming, promotion, and public relations is necessary to be successful at this job. Average base salary is about $180,000. Some in major markets earn from $100,000 to $250,000.

Human Resources Manager

Persons in this job recruit and interview job applicants, explain company policies and benefits to new employees, and respond to complaints and problems that employees raise. They prepare reports required by the Equal Employment Opportunity Commission (EEOC), the Occupational Safety and Health Administration (OSHA), and the Federal Communications Commission (FCC). The human resources manager also advises management on personnel matters. The program director or business manager may handle these duties.

Business Manager/Controller

This person supervises the accounting department and is responsible for collecting and paying bills, issuing salary checks, assisting department heads in budget preparation, and compiling financial information and reports for management. He or she maintains the station's licenses, public inspection files, and official logs. In most locations the business manager also supervises the stockroom, telephone service, purchasing of supplies, and station security.

Educational requirements are college training in business administration and accounting. Salaries vary with size of operation. The national average is about $47,000. Large-market stations pay between $50,000 to $170,000.

Traffic

The traffic department has been called the "paperwork heart" of a radio station. It is the repository and processing center for records of all commercial accounts, public service messages, programs, and features. Traffic prepares the daily broadcast schedule and provides performance reports for billing purposes. Most traffic departments are computerized operations.

Radio Traffic Manager/Supervisor

This employee prepares a minute-by-minute list of all programs and commercials to be aired each day and maintains a record of the time that every segment was broadcast or omitted. This job requires business training, computer skills, and a methodical mind. Average small-market salary is about $20,000. Large stations pay $25,000 to $35,000.

Radio Traffic Assistant

Where program and commercial activity is heavy, one or more traffic assistants may share the workload. For example, in combined AM-FM operations, one person handles AM traffic and another handles FM traffic.

Engineering

Every radio station must have at least one licensed chief engineer who is responsible for periodically inspecting, repairing, and maintaining the broadcast equipment. This person need not be a full-time employee but must work the number of hours necessary to fully perform the prescribed duties.

Each station is also required to have a licensed operator on hand to monitor the transmitter during all hours of operation. Most stations now assign this responsibility to announcers and disc jockeys who have an operator license.

With heavy automation and little need for a full-time engineer, many stations now employ a chief engineer on contract to provide whatever inspections and services are required. Licensed station personnel handle other technical duties.

Full-time radio chief engineers have average earnings of $50,000, but larger AM and FM stations pay considerably more. Contract engineers charge about $12,000 annually to each station they serve, and they commonly work for more than one operation.

Additional Jobs in Radio

A good way to get started in broadcasting is to find employment as a receptionist or some other administrative job. Basic educational requirements are a high school diploma and some business school training or former employment in office services. With more education you may be able to advance to a better job.

Most radio stations in the United States and Canada have small staffs and depend on "combo" employees to do two or more different daily jobs. Your chances of getting hired for such work will depend on how skilled and versatile you are.

These are some typical combo positions: disc jockey/technician, announcer/newscaster, sportscaster/sales, receptionist/traffic, secretary/bookkeeper, reporter/newscaster/producer.

Some stations hire temporary help when needed and pay hourly wages, but they provide no company benefits. Quite a few AM and FM stations use part-time employees for fewer than 40 hours a week to handle a specific shift or assignment. Amount of compensation varies according to the nature of the work and the experience of the employee.

11

Careers Related to Broadcasting

When we think of broadcast careers, most of us picture the worlds of television, radio, and cable. But these aren't the only areas where skills and education in broadcasting can be put to good use. Corporate video production, independent video production, video postproduction, advertising, video for nonprofits—all these areas and more are open to talented and interested individuals.

Nonbroadcast Video Systems

Thousands of businesses and institutions have their own broadcasting studios and video systems that they use to create and transmit various kinds of programming to specific audiences at one or more locations. Company officials often appear on camera from national headquarters and address employees or stockholders in a number of cities. Simpler types of audio and video equipment are widely used to feed music, announcements, or visual presentations to multiple stores.

Former broadcasters often like working as managers, producers, and performers for these narrowcasting facilities because they provide good salaries, pleasant working conditions, job stability, and minimal worry about deadlines and audience ratings.

This field of opportunity—which is often referred to as corporate video or nonbroadcast video—has been likened to employment at a small-market television station. The audience is limited in size and so is the communications system. A few staff members handle many different duties. The director also may serve as scriptwriter, lighting engineer, and cameraperson. It's a great place to gain experience, and many young men and women advance from such jobs to bigger and better ones.

Video systems employ far more people than all the radio and television stations in the United States and Canada. Owners of video systems include educational institutions, hospitals, government agencies, museums, independent producers, postproduction studios, and professional associations. Video system productions include everything from feature-length movies and TV commercials to training films, slides, and sales promotion materials.

Video systems jobs include:

Video Manager

The video manager is responsible for overall management of an audiovisual department. He or she approves staff and salaries. Qualifications include administrative experience, working knowledge of budgets, and an understanding of the latest communications technology. Typical salary is about $50,000 to $60,000.

Operations Manager

This person supervises a media department or studio. He or she coordinates scheduling of audiovisual productions. The supervisor also recommends annual budgets, staff changes, and salary adjustments. Average salary is $40,000 to $50,000.

Video Coordinator

This multitalented individual handles all the creative, technical, production, and management responsibilities for a small facility. Salary range is $30,000 to $60,000.

Corporate Communications Producer

This position coordinates all aspects of an assigned video production. The producer is responsible for determining the objectives to be achieved and assembling the necessary creative and technical personnel. The producer then oversees the project to complete it on time and within budget. Typical starting salary is $30,000.

Assistant Producer

The assistant producer helps to carry out all of the producer's objectives and duties. This person also may serve as a writer. Salary range is $20,000 to $30,000.

Director

The director selects and directs the talent and technical crew in creating an actual production on location or in a studio. Typical starting salary is $25,000.

Production Assistant

The production assistant helps the director change sets, adjust lighting, revise scripts, or provide any other help that is needed. Typical salary is about $24,000.

Writer

A writer evaluates and interprets the client's needs, researches source materials, and develops scripts for production. Typical starting salary range is $25,000 to $30,000.

Audio/Video Specialist

This person has a thorough knowledge of electronic media and is capable of setting up media programs and installations. He or she can also troubleshoot equipment problems. Entry-level salary range is $25,000 to $30,000.

Chief Video Specialist

This professional is an engineer and is responsible for the technical performance of video and audio recording, switching, and distribution equipment. He or she installs, tests, and evaluates electronic devices. This position also reviews new developments in equipment and techniques. Starting salary range is $25,000 to $30,000.

Technician

A technician serves as a technical member of an audio, video, or film crew. To qualify you must be capable of operating and maintaining electronic equipment. Salary range is from $25,000 to $45,000.

Sales and Marketing

Sales and marketing personnel are responsible for selling and marketing audio/video programs, products, or services. Typical first-year earnings are $25,000.

Professor/Instructor

A full-time teacher of electronic communications subjects works at a college, university, or other school system. Salary is approximately $35,000.

Video Production

Commercial video production in the United States and Canada generates more than $30 billion in revenues annually. The biggest share of this comes from producing spots and color graphics, but the output includes hundreds of informational and entertainment presentations that include everything from TV programs and feature films to brief commercial and public service announcements.

You will find dozens of video producers and video production studios in most large cities, but they are in many smaller communities as well. In addition, some 12,000 part-time operations in TV stations, cable systems, and various public and private organizations make this dynamic industry a large employer of skilled communicators.

The number of postproduction houses is also growing. They specialize in enhancing the aural and visual elements of a video presentation—such as voiceovers, music, sound effects, titles, and graphics—to create the finished product.

Principal clients of postproduction houses are advertising agencies, contract producers, and corporations, which require assistance in completing TV commercials, feature films, music videos, and other audio/video presentations.

Most job opportunities in this field call for creative and artistic talent, plus a working knowledge of audio/video recorders, editing equipment, monitors, and computers. On-the-job training is the best way to gain such experience.

Video production jobs include:

Office Manager

A manager supervises the day-to-day operations of a production company and serves as the top administrator. In small operations, this person may also act as a business manager, writer, and producer. He or she should combine creative and management capabilities and have experience in electronic media. A college degree is helpful. Salary range is $50,000 to $100,000.

Administrative Assistant

This person assists the manager with correspondence, community relations, record keeping, and overall supervision of personnel and operations. In small organizations, he or she may also serve as a receptionist and bookkeeper. The job requires a college education and media experience. Salary is approximately $26,000.

Sales and Marketing Manager

This manager develops and coordinates the company's sales and marketing efforts to obtain as many business clients as possible. He or she supervises the sales staff. In small operations, the marketing manager also may write and produce materials. Requirements are a degree in marketing, advertising, or communications. Media sales experience is a plus. Base salary range is $45,000 to $85,000.

Account Executive

An account executive makes sales calls to obtain new business and services existing accounts. A college degree is preferred, plus sales training and experience. Compensation is $30,000 to $75,000.

Marketing and Sales Assistant

This position provides assistance to the sales manager and account executives. The job involves maintaining records of all business transactions and sales activity. To qualify you must be a high school graduate, but a college degree is preferred. You should have sales potential and computer skills. Salary range is $20,000 to $35,000.

Production Manager

This person is responsible for all studio production and supervision of production staff. In small operations this job may include creative production duties. Requirements are a degree in communications and several years of TV production experience. Salary range is $45,000 to $90,000.

Producer-Director

The producer-director develops and directs video productions to meet the needs and specifications of individual clients—anything from a 15-second TV commercial to feature-length movies for television. Requirements include a degree in broadcasting or theater and TV production experience. Salary range is $35,000 to $55,000.

Scriptwriter

A scriptwriter is responsible for transforming the client's wishes into a visually oriented script that includes narration dialogue and camera instructions. He or she then makes the necessary changes called for during the production. The position requires a college degree and proven writing skills. Many writers work on a freelance basis and are paid by the assignment. A full-time scriptwriter usually doubles as a producer-director. Compensation range is $25,000 to $65,000.

Videographer

This person shoots and edits tape or film at a production studio. He or she works under the supervision of a producer or director and uses appropriate cameras, lenses, and lighting equipment. To qualify you should be educated and experienced in cinematography. Pay averages $20 to $40 per hour.

Video Postproduction Jobs

The following positions exist in postproduction facilities. It is here that visual and audio elements are combined and video presentations are edited into their final form. These employees are generally recruited from TV stations or other production studios where they have gained experience with editing equipment and character generators.

Postproduction jobs include:

Off-Line Editor

This person works in an editing suite and does the initial major editing of video or film footage. Skilled video editors are in demand for both freelance work and full-time positions. Salary range is $40,000 to $75,000.

Online Editor

An online editor works with clients to edit a video production into its final form. He or she operates computers and technical machines to integrate and coordinate the desired components. Salary range is $40,000 to $85,000.

Assistant Editor

This person sets up editing machines and character generators for use by the editor. The assistant editor keeps track of reels and logs and provides help wherever needed. Salary range is $35,000 to $50,000.

Audio Engineer

This sound specialist does the final blending and balancing of voiceovers, sound effects, and music into the finished video production. Prerequisites are technical training and audio-engineering experience. Pay range is $20 to $40 an hour.

Maintenance Engineer

The maintenance engineer is responsible for keeping the studio's technical equipment in working order. The job requires technical training and experience and problem-solving skills. Pay averages $15 to $20 an hour. Duplication engineers earn about $15 an hour.

Telecine Colorist

This person specializes in maximizing the color potential of a production. He or she uses computer equipment to equalize and enhance video transferred from film and tapes of varying color intensity. The position requires a high degree of artistic and technical talent. Pay is $75,000 to $100,000 or more.

Additional Fields

Every year, thousands of students at colleges, universities, and trade schools take courses in electronic communications. Many of them would like to be broadcasters, but the number of applicants outweighs the number of available positions in the television, radio, and cable industries. Fortunately, employment can be found in other areas that require a trained broadcaster's skills.

Knowledge of broadcasting has helped many students obtain good positions in advertising, marketing, fund-raising, promotion, publicity, and public relations. Many governmental, religious, cultural, and social service agencies hire communications experts to keep the public informed about their activities or provide leadership in fund-raising. So finding work as an electronic media professional should be relatively easy, provided you are adequately prepared and willing to work in a broadcast-related field.

Sales Representatives

Most commercial broadcasting facilities are affiliated with sales organizations that maintain offices in principal cities and sell out-of-town advertising time for their client stations. Sales representatives deal mainly with national and regional advertisers. To be successful, you should love to sell and do it in a smart, aggressive, and pleasing manner. Commissions and earnings are high for those who work long hours, but competition for sales jobs is keen. Some firms engage in program production, own broadcast properties, and employ specialists in research, marketing, programming, and promotion.

Advertising, Marketing, Promotions, Public Relations, and Sales Managers

Like most businesses, the broadcast industry is as concerned as any other with turning a profit. To that end, emphasis is placed on advertising, marketing, promotions, public relations, and sales professionals to drive revenue.

Employment in these areas is expected to increase sharply through 2010, but the competition for spots within media organizations will be tough given the high salaries these employees can earn.

Duties for advertising, marketing, promotions, public relations, and sales managers include developing marketing strategies, conducting market research, developing products, and setting prices. In small companies, one person—typically the owner or CEO—may be responsible for all of these. Larger firms employ a staff that a manager oversees.

According to recent statistics, more than 707,000 advertising, marketing, promotions, public relations, and sales managers were employed in the United States, 38 percent of which worked more than 50 hours per week. Professionals in these areas are often subjected to long hours and work under the pressures of deadlines and sales quotas. Travel to industry meetings or to meet with clients is also common, adding to the hectic pace.

Public Information Officer

Most large public and private organizations employ one or more professional communicators to prepare and disseminate news and press releases, edit publications, reply to requests and questions from the public, and cultivate media contacts. The position, commonly known as a public information officer (PIO) or spokesperson, requires communications skills and knowledge of journalism practices, publicity, and public relations.

Applicants with electronic media education and experience are frequently favored for this job. Anyone who likes this type of work and does it well can make it a launching pad to higher levels of management and compensation.

Nonprofit Organizations

Employment opportunities for specialists in radio, television, and Internet communications are plentiful among nonprofit organizations. Included in this vast panorama of enterprises are large numbers of charities and social service agencies including medical research labs, educational institutions, and religious, governmental, social, and political-action groups.

Altogether more than one million organizations employ more than eight million people and disseminate billions of dollars annually to various causes. Many employees prefer to work for a nonprofit agency because there's usually less stress and competitive pressure than in a for-profit business. Salaries, however, are often less than those paid in the private sector.

12

OPPORTUNITIES IN BROADCASTING FOR WOMEN AND MINORITIES

ACCORDING TO THE Bureau of Labor Statistics, although whites and males held a majority of high-ranking managerial positions in the broadcast industry in recent years, minorities (defined as African-Americans, Latinos, and Asians) made some progress in achieving a more level playing field (see Tables 12.1 and 12.2).

Between 1995 and 2000, minority representation in managerial positions increased from 14.9 percent to 16.5 percent, reaching a high of 16.8 percent in 1998. Representation in technician-related jobs increased from 23 percent to 30.6 percent in the same period.

The opposite was true for minorities in sales positions, as their numbers dropped from 41.8 percent in 1995 to 29.8 percent in 2000.

The number of women in the broadcast industry between 1995 and 2000 showed little improvement. Official and manager-level positions increased slightly, rising from 40.8 percent in 1995 to 41.6 percent in 2000. Women's numbers decreased slightly in technician jobs and showed mixed results among sales workers and professionals.

More recently, however, the Radio-Television News Directors Association and Foundation found that despite continued strides by women into managerial positions, nearly all numbers for minorities in the television and radio industries decreased in 2003 for the second year in a row.

Minority representation in television news sank from 20.6 percent in 2002 to 18.1 percent in 2003. This compares with the 12.5 percent of minorities working at newspapers. The number of female television news directors reached its highest point ever in 2003, with 26.5 percent occupying those positions. This figure was a slight increase over the previous year's number of 25.9 percent.

Table 12.1 Broadcast News Workforce

	2003	2002	2001	1994
Television				
Caucasian	81.9%	79.4%	75.4%	82.9%
African-American	8.4	9.3	9.9	10.1
Latino	6.5	7.7	10.1	4.2
Asian-American	2.7	3.1	4.1	2.2
Native American	0.5	0.5	0.6	0.6
Radio				
Caucasian	93.5%	92.0%	89.3%	85.3%
African-American	4.8	4.1	5.2	5.7
Latino	1.2	2.4	5.5	4.2
Asian-American	0.3	0.8	<1.0	0.6
Native American	0.2	0.7	<1.0	1.0

Source: 2003 RTNDA/Ball State University Annual Survey: Women and Minorities: One Step Forward and Two Steps Back

Table 12.2 Broadcast News Directors

	2003	*2002*	*2001*	*1994*
Television				
Caucasian	93.4%	90.8%	92.0%	92.1%
African-American	0.9	2.0	0.6	1.6
Latino	4.4	5.8	5.7	3.8
Asian-American	0.9	0.4	1.1	1.5
Native American	0.4	1.0	0.6	1.0
Radio				
Caucasian	95.0%	94.9%	95.6%	91.4%
African-American	2.5	1.9	1.5	5.4
Latino	1.7	2.6	2.9	2.4
Asian American	0	0	<1.0	0
Native American	0.8	0.6	<1.0	0.8

Source: 2003 RTNDA/Ball State University Annual Survey: Women and Minorities: One Step Forward and Two Steps Back

Gender Salary Comparison

Although the salary gap between male and female employees is narrowing, a 1997 survey conducted by Women in Cable and Telecommunications Foundation showed that female professionals in cable, DBS, and wireless cable companies earned an average annual salary of $50,378. Men in similar jobs earned $59,354.

Entry-level salaries for women was $26,064, only 3 percent less than for men. Differences in pay are more pronounced at upper management levels. Female supervisors in cable earned an average salary of $31,860, which was 25 percent less than that received by men. Similar but smaller gaps of 10 percent to 11 percent are common in radio, TV, public relations, and advertising.

More recently, the Women in Cable and Telecommunications Foundation found in a 2003 study that 36 percent of companies surveyed had enacted policies to address equal pay for equal work. In addition, nearly one-third of companies surveyed had addressed individual cases of pay inequity between men and women.

Minority Ownership in Broadcasting

Although the Federal Communications Commission does not require broadcast licensees to identify their race or ethnicity, the Minority Telecommunications Development Program in the Department of Commerce annually collects information from various periodicals and other sources regarding minority ownership of radio and television stations.

According to the Department of Commerce, as of 2000, minorities owned 449 commercial radio and television broadcast properties, which represented 3.8 percent of all the stations in the country. This compares with 305 stations in 1998, which represented 2.9 percent of the industry total. African-Americans comprised the largest group of minority broadcast station owners with 211 radio and television stations. That figure represented one-half of all minority ownership and was a 15 percent increase compared with 1998. Hispanics owned 187 stations in 2000, which represented 44 percent of the minority ownership total.

A Final Word

Although consolidation of station ownership has eliminated some radio and TV jobs, it has also created quite a few new ones. Instead of working for one radio or TV station, you may qualify to represent a group of stations as an account executive or a specialist in news, programming, production, marketing, engineering, or research. Multiple-station owners encourage intermarket programming, syndication purchases, and the creation of mini-networks and special events. As a result, qualified individuals are sought for these high-salaried positions.

Whether you attend college, a trade school, or go into the armed forces or directly into the electronic media workplace, you will need training and aptitude in the use of sophisticated communications devices. Employers are requiring job seekers to be computer literate and technically adept. To achieve your maximum potential, you also will need a well-rounded education that exposes you to significant historical and current ideas and teaches you how to comprehend and communicate what you see and hear.

Students who are unable to leave home can use computers and cable connections to take courses, plug into library resources, and participate in classroom discussions.

Whatever broadcast path you choose, concentrate on increasing your knowledge and technical capabilities. Look for better ways to do things. Remember, the challenges that lie ahead may appear awesome, but so are the possibilities. In this age of remarkable new communications technology, those who are best prepared will reap the greatest rewards.

With the entire universe as your workplace, a new generation of broadcasters and narrowcasters has an unlimited number of major topics to explore. But despite technological advancements that have greatly magnified our ability to reach and inform people, no comparable breakthrough has occurred in the art of communications. That still requires a consistent and sincere human effort to understand others and make oneself understood.

To speak clearly and constructively about significant issues and ideas, communicators must be better educated, more sensitive, and more resourceful than their predecessors. They must be dedicated to serving the needs and interests of the public and conscious of their responsibility to be relevant, dependable, and fair.

Perhaps such serious responsibilities and bright possibilities will entice you to become an electronic media professional and join the ranks of tomorrow's communications leaders.

Appendix A

Scholarships, Internships, Fellowships, and Grants

ANYONE CONTEMPLATING A career in electronic media should consider a college education as necessary preparation. Help-wanted ads for broadcasters and narrowcasters frequently specify that applicants must have a degree in communications plus professional experience.

Although attending an institution of higher learning has become quite expensive, this doesn't necessarily mean you can't afford to earn a degree. Thousands of students receive financial aid through scholarships, internships, fellowships, and grants offered by organizations such as the following:

- **American Women in Radio and Television.** Offers local scholarship programs and internships. More information can be found at awrt.org.
- **Asian-American Journalists Association.** More than 300 students have been awarded over $420,000 in scholarships

since the AAJA was founded in 1981. Sponsors include the
S. I. Newhouse Foundation and the Freedom Forum. For
more information visit aaja.org.

- **Broadcast Education Association.** BEA awards 15 scholarships to juniors, seniors, and graduate students at BEA
member universities each year (listed in Appendix C). For
additional information visit beaweb.org/scholar1.html.
- **California Chicano News Media Association.** Lists broadcasting and print internships across the United States. Visit
ccnma.org.
- **Chips Quinn Scholars.** Provides training, internships, and
$1,000 scholarships to college students of color who are
pursuing careers in journalism. Go to chipsquinn.org.
- **Corporation for Public Broadcasting.** Information is
available at cpb.org.
- **The Fulbright Scholar Program.** Provides grants to broadcasting professionals and communications faculty to teach
and conduct research in 140 countries worldwide. Grants
can be awarded in three-month increments up to an
academic year or longer. Eligibility information and
application materials are available at cies.org.
- **International Radio and Television Society.** Allows those
seeking a career in communications to develop many skills
required for the field. Go to irts.org.
- **International Radio and Television Society Foundation.**
Teaches promising communicators the ins and outs of the
business world. Interested students can visit irts.org.
- **The John Bayliss Broadcast Foundation.** Offers up to 20
scholarships worth $5,000 each to outstanding college
students pursuing a career in radio. More information is
available at baylissfoundation.org.

- **LinTV.** Offers scholarship and training program for minority candidates. Visit lintv.com.
- **National Association of Black Journalists.** Awards scholarships, internships, and fellowships. Visit nabj.org/scholar.html.
- **NAB Grants for Research in Broadcasting.** Each year the National Association of Broadcasters allows academic personnel, graduate students, and senior undergraduates to compete for $25,000. The funds are usually delivered in the form of four awards and six grants. Applications are available at nab.org/research/grants/grants.asp.
- **The NABEF Professional Fellowship Program.** Provides a total of four up-and-coming radio and television broadcasters with management training. Increasing diversity and promoting minorities in the broadcast industry is of particular importance. Go to nabef.org.
- **National Association of Hispanic Journalists.** Offers several different scholarships. For more information go to nahj.org.
- **National Association of Minority Media Executives.** This organization offers six fellowships and is made up of professionals of color who work across the media industry. NAMME exists, in part, to encourage diversity in media management ranks of the media industry. Applications and further information are available at namme.org.
- **National Gay and Lesbian Task Force.** Messenger-Anderson Scholarship and internship program for high school seniors and undergraduate college students who plan to pursue a degree in journalism. Go to ngltf.org.
- **National Public Radio.** Internship program for students interested in a career in public radio. Log on to npr.org.

- **Native American Journalists Association.** Offers a variety of scholarships. More information can be found at naja.com.
- **Public Broadcasting Service.** Internship opportunities with various local PBS stations can be found at pbs.org/stations.
- **Radio-Television News Directors Association and Foundation.** Internship and scholarship opportunities for aspiring journalists can be found at rtnda.org.
- **Society of Professional Journalists.** Sponsors several awards, fellowships, and internships. For more information visit http://spj.org/awards.
- **TV Jobs.** Internships at networks, broadcast stations, and other settings across the country. Visit tvjobs.com/intern .htm for details. Scholarship information can be found at tvjobs.com/scholar.htm.
- **WBZ Radio and TV.** CBS-owned stations that offer internships to college sophomores, juniors, seniors, and graduate students can be found at wbz.com.
- **WCVB TV.** Offers many internship opportunities and the Leo L. Beranek Fellowship for News Reporting. Log on to wcvb.com.

Many state broadcasting associations provide scholarship and internship assistance, as well as job listings.

Alabama
al-broadcasters.org/jobbank.html

Arkansas
arkbroadcasters.org

Arizona
azbroadcasters.org

California
cabroadcasters.org

Florida
 fab.org/tvjobs.shtml

Georgia
 gab.org

Illinois
 ilba.org

Indiana
 indianabroadcasters.org

Iowa
 iowabroadcasters.com

Kansas
 kab.net/jobbank

Kentucky
 kba.org

Louisiana
 broadcasters.org

Maine
 mab.org

Maryland, Washington, D.C., and Delaware
 mdcd.com

Massachusetts
 massbroadcasters.org

Michigan
 michmab.com

Minnesota
 minnesotabroadcasters.com

Missouri
 mbaweb.org

Nevada
 nevadabroadcasters.org

New Hampshire
 nhab.org

New Mexico
 nmba.org

New York
 nysbroadcastersassn.org

North Carolina
 ncbroadcast.com/job-bank.html

North Dakota
 ndba.org/jobbank.htm

Oklahoma
 oabok.org/jobbank.html

Oregon
 theoab.org

Tennessee
 tabtn.org

Texas
 tab.org

Vermont
vab.org/jobs_page.html

Virginia
vab.net

West Virginia
wvba.com/jobs.htm

Wisconsin
wi-broadcasters.org/jobs/
toc.htm

Wyoming
wyomingbroadcasting.org

Appendix B

Broadcasting and Journalism Job Banks

Log on to the following websites for more information and jobs in broadcasting and journalism.

Asia Pacific Broadcasting, apb-news.com
Asian-American Journalists Association, aaja.org
Birschbach Recruitment Network, mediarecruiter.com
Black Broadcasters Alliance, thebba.org
Broadcast Cable Financial Management Association,
    bcfm.com/job_bank/general_information.asp
California Chicano News Media Association, ccnma.org
Don Fitzpatrick Associates, tvspy.com/jobs.htm
EmployNow, employnow.com
Investigative Reporters and Editors, http://ire.org/jobs
Mandy's International Film and Television, mandy.com
Maslow Media Group, maslowmedia.com
Media Staffing Network, mediastaffingnetwork.com
MediaLine, medialine.com
National Association of Black Journalists, nabj.org

National Association of Television Program, natpe.org

National Diversity Newspaper Job Bank,
    http://newsjobs.com/home.html

Radio-Television News Directors Association and
    Foundation, rtnda.org

Society of Broadcast Engineers, sbe.org

Talent Dynamics, talentdynamics.com/jobs/index.html

TV Jobs, tvjobs.com/jbcenter.htm

TV and Radio Jobs, tvandradiojobs.com

TV Rundown, tvrundown.com/resource.html

Appendix C

Colleges and Universities

THE FOLLOWING COLLEGES and universities were institutional members of the Broadcast Education Association in 2003 and 2004:

Alabama

University of Alabama, tcf.ua.edu

Arizona

Arizona State University, asu.edu/cronkite
Northern Arizona University, comm.nau.edu
Yavapai College Sedona Center for Arts and Technology,
dstory.com/dsfsedona_04

Arkansas

Arkansas State University, http://comm.astate.edu
Harding University, harding.edu/communication
John Brown University, jbu.edu/academics/communication

University of Arkansas, uark.edu/depts/jourinfo/public_html
University of the Ozarks,
   ozarks.edu/academics/bcg/communications.html

California

Azusa Pacific University, apu.edu/clas/commstudies
California State University (Chico), csuchico.edu/cme
California State University (Fresno), csufresno.edu/comm
California State University (Fullerton), http://communications
   .fullerton.edu
California State University (Northridge), cinemaandtelevision.com
Citrus College, citruscollege.edu
City College of San Francisco, ccsf.edu/departments/
   ed_programs.html
Cosumnes River College, crc.losrios.edu/areasofstudy/c/
   comm_media/comm_media.htm
Golden West College, http://gwc.info
Humboldt State University, humboldt.edu/~jnhsu
Mount San Antonio College, mtsac.edu
Palomar College, palomar.edu/communications
Pepperdine University, seaver.pepperdine.edu/communication/
   academics/communication.htm
Point Loma Nazarene University, ptloma.edu/communication
San Francisco State University, sfsu.edu/~puboff/programs/
   undergrad/beca.htm
San Jose State University, tvradiofilmtheatre.com
Santa Ana College/Santiago Canyon College, sccollege.edu/tv
University of LaVerne, ulaverne.edu
University of San Francisco, http://artsci.usfca.edu/servlet/
   deptwelcome?deptid=14
University of Southern California, http://ascweb.usc.edu/home.php

Colorado

Colorado State University, colostate.edu/depts/speech
University of Colorado (Boulder), colorado.edu/journalism
University of Denver, http://soc.du.edu

District of Columbia

American University, soc.american.edu
George Washington University, gwu.edu/~bulletin/ugrad/
emda.html
Howard University, howard.edu/schoolcommunications

Florida

Art Institute of Fort Lauderdale, aifl.artinstitutes.edu/programs.asp
Barry University, barry.edu/communication/default.htm
Florida A&M University, famu.edu
Florida International University, http://jmc.fiu.edu/sjmc
Florida State University, fsu.edu/~film/main.html
University of Central Florida, cas.ucf.edu/communication
University of Miami, miami.edu/com

Georgia

Augusta State University, aug.edu/langlitcom
University of Georgia, grady.uga.edu
Valdosta State University, valdosta.edu

Hawaii

University of Hawaii, hawaii.edu

Idaho

Brigham Young University, byui.edu

Illinois

Bradley University, http://admissions.bradley.edu/programsofstudy/
cfa-com.php
College of St. Francis, stfrancis.edu/admissions/academics/
masscom.htm
Eastern Illinois University, eiu.edu
Illinois Institute of Technology, iit.edu
Illinois State University, communication.ilstu.edu/default.htm
North Central College, noctrl.edu/academics/departments/
speech_communication_theatre/index.shtml
Northwestern University, medill.northwestern.edu
Prairie State College, prairie.cc.il.us
Principia College, prin.edu/college/academics/departments/
mass_comm/index.htm
Rock Valley College, rockvalleycollege.edu/show.cfm?durki=526
Roosevelt University, roosevelt.edu/cas/comm/default.htm
Saint Xavier University, sxu.edu/communication
South Suburban College, ssc.cc.il.us
Southern Illinois University Edwardsville, siue.edu/masscomm
Western Illinois University, wiu.edu/comm

Indiana

Ball State University, bsu.edu/cim
Butler University, butler.edu/mediaarts
DePauw University, depauw.edu/acad/communication
Indiana State University, indstate.edu/comm
Indiana University, indiana.edu/~telecom

Manchester College, manchester.edu/academics/departments/
communication/index.htm
Purdue University (Calumet), calumet.purdue.edu/cca
University of Indianapolis, http://communication.uindy.edu
Vincennes University, vinu.edu

Iowa

Dordt College, dordt.edu/academics/programs/communication
Drake University, drake.edu/journalism/sjmc.html
University of Iowa, uiowa.edu/~journal
University of Northern Iowa, chfa.uni.edu/comstudy
Wartburg College, wartburg.edu/commarts/ca.html

Kansas

Fort Hays State University, fhsu.edu/int
Kansas State University, http://jmc.ksu.edu
Pittsburg State University, pittstate.edu/comm
Washburn University, washburn.edu/cas/massmedia

Kentucky

Morehead State University, moreheadstate.edu/colleges/humanities/
communications
Murray State University, mursuky.edu/qacd/cfac/jmc/index.html
University of Kentucky, uky.edu/comminfostudies/jat

Louisiana

Grambling State University, gram.edu
Louisiana College, lacollege.edu/arts/commarts_dept.html
Louisiana State University, manship.lsu.edu

Loyola University New Orleans, http://cas.loyno.edu/
   communications
McNeese State University, mcneese.edu/colleges/lib/deptmass/
   index.asp
University of Louisiana (Monroe), ulm.edu/communication

Maine

Southern Maine Technical College, smccme.edu
St. Joseph's College, sjcme.edu

Maryland

Columbia Union College, cuc.edu/academic/departments/
   commjournal/index.html
Montgomery College, montgomerycollege.edu/departments/itv
Towson University, towson.edu/emf

Massachusetts

Boston University, bu.edu/com/communication.html
Emerson College, emerson.edu/school_of_communication
Mount Ida College, mountida.edu/sp.cfm?pageid=339
University of Massachusetts, umass.edu/communication/
   undergraduate/the_major/index.shtml

Michigan

Central Michigan University, ccfa.cmich.edu
Eastern Michigan University, emich.edu/public/cta
Ferris State University, ferris.edu/htmls/fsucatlg/coursecatalog/
   programs.cfm
Michigan State University, http://cas.msu.edu
Wayne State University, wayne.edu

Minnesota

Bethany Lutheran College, blc.edu
Northwestern College, nwc.edu
University of Minnesota, catalogs.umn.edu/ug/cla/cla72.html
University of St. Thomas, stthomas.edu

Mississippi

Mississippi State University, msstate.edu/dept/communication
University of Southern Mississippi, usm.edu/mcj

Missouri

Evangel University, evangel.edu/academics/communication
Missouri Southern State University (Joplin) mssu.edu/comm/
home.htm
Southeast Missouri State University, semo.edu/study/masscomm/
index.htm
Southwest Missouri State University, http://mjf.smsu.edu
Stephens College, stephens.edu/academics/programs/communication
Truman State University, http://ll.truman.edu
Webster University, webster.edu/depts/comm

Montana

University of Montana, www2.umt.edu/rtv/default.htm

Nebraska

Creighton University, http://jmc.creighton.edu
University of Nebraska (Kearney), unk.edu/acad/comm/home.html
University of Nebraska (Omaha), http://communication
.unomaha.edu

Nevada

University of Nevada (Las Vegas), unlv.edu/colleges/greenspun
University of Nevada (Reno), unr.edu/journalism

New Jersey

Montclair State University, montclair.edu/pages/commstudies/
commstudies.html
Rowan University, rowan.edu/elan/communic/ncommhom.htm

New York

Brooklyn College—CUNY, bctvr.org
Buffalo State College, buffalostate.edu/depts/communication
C.W. Post Campus, LIU, liu.edu/~svpa
Hofstra University, hofstra.edu
Marist College, marist.edu/commarts
St. John's University, sbu.edu/academics_journalism.html
SUNY (Brockport), brockport.edu/cmc
Syracuse University, http://newhouse.syr.edu

North Carolina

Appalachian State University, appstate.edu
University of North Carolina (Greensboro), uncg.edu/cst
University of North Carolina (Wilmington), uncwil.edu/com
Wake Forest University, wfu.edu/academics/communication

North Dakota

University of North Dakota, und.edu/dept/scomm

Ohio

Bowling Green State University, bgsu.edu/departments/tcom
Case Western Reserve University, cwru.edu
Franciscan University of Steubenville, franciscan.edu
International College of Broadcasting, icbcollege.com
John Carroll University, jcu.edu/communications
Muskingum College, http://fates.cns.muskingum.edu/external/
   academics/facultymain.html
Ohio University, tcomschool.ohiou.edu
Otterbein College, otterbein.edu/dept/comm/index.htm
University of Akron, www3.uakron.edu/schlcomm/page/index.htm
University of Cincinnati, http://asweb.artsci.uc.edu/
   communication/index.htm
University of Dayton, http://artssciences.udayton.edu/
   communication
Xavier University, xavier.edu/communication_arts

Oklahoma

Cameron University, cameron.edu/academic/liberal_arts/
   communications/index.html
Northwestern Oklahoma State University, nwosu.edu/
   communication/index.html
Oklahoma Baptist University, okbu.edu
Oklahoma City University, okcu.edu/petree/humanities/
   mass_comm
Oklahoma State University, http://ok4h.fourh.dasnr.okstate.edu/sjb/
   sjbindex.php
Oral Roberts University, oru.edu/university/departments/schools/
   arts/commarts

Southeastern Oklahoma State University, sosu.edu/departments/communications

University of Central Oklahoma, libarts.ucok.edu/dept/communications/index.asp

University of Oklahoma, http://jmc.ou.edu

Pennsylvania

College Misericordia, misericordia.edu/templates/alltemps.cfm?cat_id=297&pg=1

Duquesne University, communication.duq.edu

La Salle University, lasalle.edu/academ/commun/home.htm

Pennsylvania State University, psu.edu

Shippensburg University, ship.edu/~commjour

Slippery Rock University, sru.edu

Susquehanna University, susqu.edu/ahc

Temple University, temple.edu/scatwestminster college, westminster.edu

Wilkes University, wilkes.edu/academics/sscomm/comm.asp

South Carolina

University of South Carolina, jour.sc.edu

Winthrop University, winthrop.edu/masscomm

Tennessee

Belmont University, belmont.edu

Lee University, http://flame.leeuniversity.edu/communication

Middle Tennessee State University, mtsu.edu/~masscomm

Tennessee State University, tnstate.edu

University of Tennessee (Chattanooga), utc.edu/commdept

University of Tennessee (Knoxville), http://excellent.com.utk.edu

University of Tennessee (Martin), utm.edu/departments/comm/
comm.htm

Texas

Baylor University, baylor.edu/comm_studies
Central Texas College, ctcd.cc.tx.us
Navarro College, nav.cc.tx.us
Prairie View A&M University, pvamu.edu/gridold/lang_com/
index.html
Sam Houston State University, shsu.edu/~com_www
San Antonio College, accd.edu/sac/sacmain/sac.htm
Stephen F. Austin State University, sfasu.edu/aas/comm
Texas A&M University, http://journalism.tamu.edu
Texas Christian University, communication.tcu.edu
Texas State University (San Marcos), txstate.edu
Texas Tech University, mcom.ttu.edu
Trinity University, trinity.edu/departments/communication/
index.html
University of Houston, uh.edu/academics/catalog/las/
las_degree_comm.html
University of the Incarnate Word, uiwtx.edu/~commarts
University of North Texas, unt.edu
University of Texas (Arlington), uta.edu/communication
University of Texas (Austin), http://communication.utexas.edu
University of Texas (El Paso), utep.edu/comm

Utah

Brigham Young University, http://cfac.byu.edu
University of Utah, hum.utah.edu/communication
Utah State University, usu.edu/communic

Virginia

Hampton University, hamptonu.edu/shsjc
James Madison University, http://smad.jmu.edu
Virginia Western Community College, vw.vccs.edu/radiotv

Washington

Pacific Lutheran University, plu.edu
Washington State University, libarts.wsu.edu/communication/
comm/index.asp

West Virginia

Marshall University, marshall.edu/sojmc

Wisconsin

Madison Media Institute, madisonmedia.com
Marquette University, marquette.edu
University of Wisconsin (Eau Claire), uwec.edu/commjour
University of Wisconsin (Platteville), uwplatt.edu
University of Wisconsin (Stevens Point), uwsp.edu/comm

Wyoming

University of Wyoming, http://uwadmnweb.uwyo.edu/cmjr

About the Author

ELMO ELLIS IS widely recognized as one of the most innovative figures in the history of broadcasting. During a lengthy and distinguished career that spanned more than five decades, Mr. Ellis originated many types of local and network programs that are now commonly seen and heard on television and radio.

This vice president (emeritus) of Cox Broadcasting has held programming, production, promotion, public relations, and general management positions, and offered one of the country's first courses in TV writing and production at Emory University. He also has taught TV and radio classes at Georgia State and Oglethorpe Universities and often lectures at other schools and colleges. Students frequently seek his advice regarding careers in broadcasting.

As television grew in popularity and radio declined, Mr. Ellis wrote articles and delivered speeches, including "How to Remove the Rust from Radio." The campaign succeeded in reviving nationwide interest in radio listening, and he won a Peabody Award. Over the years he has received hundreds of national and international awards for programming, civic contributions, and broadcasting leadership.

During the celebration of radio's diamond anniversary, *Radio INK* magazine paid tribute to Mr. Ellis as being among 75 legendary broadcasters who have exerted "a distinctive and major impact" on the industry.

Mr. Ellis has served as chairman of the Radio Advertising Bureau, the National FM Radio Broadcasters Association, the NAB Radio Code Board, and the NBC Radio Affiliates. He has been president of the Georgia Association of Broadcasters, Georgia AP News Broadcasters, and the Society of Professional Journalists.

A strong supporter of broadcast education, Mr. Ellis is a trustee of Oglethorpe University and a broadcasting advisory board member at Emory University and the University of Alabama.

Mr. Ellis holds three degrees and a Phi Beta Kappa key. His books and articles have been published in the United States, Japan, Australia, Canada, and elsewhere. Mr. Ellis is prominently listed in *Who's Who* and continues to share his knowledge and experience as an author, media consultant, public speaker, and syndicated newspaper columnist.